COMMANDER'S
WILD SIDE

ALSO BY TI ADELAIDE MARTIN AND TORY McPHAIL

In the Land of Cocktails

COMMANDER'S
WILD SIDE

Bold Flavors for Fresh Ingredients

from the Great Outdoors

TI ADELAIDE MARTIN AND
TORY McPHAIL

Co-Proprietor and Executive Chef of Commander's Palace

WILLIAM MORROW
An Imprint of HarperCollins*Publishers*

COMMANDER'S WILD SIDE. Copyright © 2008 by Ti Adelaide Martin and Tory McPhail. Photographs copyright © 2008 by Michael Teranova. All rights reserved. Printed in the United States of America. No part of this book may be used or reproduced in any manner whatsoever without written permission except in the case of brief quotations embodied in critical articles and reviews. For information address HarperCollins Publishers, 10 East 53rd Street, New York, NY 10022.

HarperCollins books may be purchased for educational, business, or sales promotional use. For information please write: Special Markets Department, HarperCollins Publishers, 10 East 53rd Street, New York, NY 10022.

FIRST EDITION

Designed by Ralph Fowler

Library of Congress Cataloging-in-Publication Data has been applied for.

ISBN 978-0-06-111989-7

08 09 10 11 12 WBC/QW 10 9 8 7 6 5 4 3 2 1

I'd like to dedicate this book to my parents and family
who instilled in me a curiosity about food and its origins,
a respect for the outdoors, and a love of life.

—Tory McPhail

This book is dedicated to the extraordinary team that is
Commander's Palace. Led for twenty years by Steve Woodruff,
your enduring passion to always reinvent the Commander's experience
and to be the restaurant that all of New Orleans is proud of
inspires me every day. Two shows daily.

—Ti Adelaide Martin

Acknowledgments

I'd like to thank my good friends Chris Barbato and Tom Robey for helping me test every single recipe on my home stove while Commander's was closed after Hurricane Katrina for thirteen months. I'd also like to thank my buddy Danny Trace, whom I've been on more hunting and fishing trips with than anyone else.

A big thank-you to Maria Wisdom, whose hard work and perfectionism made these recipes endlessly easier to read and cook.

Most of all, I'd like to acknowledge my mentor Jamie Shannon for giving me the passion to succeed on this level, which I'd give up ten times over to have him back.

—Tory McPhail

Contents

COMMANDER'S
WILD SIDE

Introduction

W E HUNT, AND WE COOK. If you do either one, this book is for you and in honor of you. We may have grown up on different coasts (Tory in the Pacific Northwest and Ti on the Gulf Coast in New Orleans), but we share similar childhoods—adventures spent on the water and in the woods, hunting and fishing. And the same passion for cooking.

Ti still dreams of crabbing with her cousins as a kid, and making marinated crab salad that night to eat with her hands. Tory will never forget the moment he saw a majestic, giant elk gliding and blinking through a snowstorm. We were both raised and surrounded by people who hunt and fish, the hobbies of choice for many Washingtonians and Louisianians. Hunting and fishing is about the sport, but also so much is about being in nature and being with friends. The crazy things that happen, the stories—it all adds up to living life fully. We work hard and we play hard, and we like that about ourselves.

Maybe it's not a coincidence that the same was true for the people who settled in Louisiana. This soupy land surrounded by water was hard to navigate and was isolated from the rest of the country for so long. This was not an easy way of life. Louisianians learned to live off the land, to adapt. Fish, deer, rabbit, alligator, duck, and goose were cooked for dinner. Rice and sugarcane were harvested. Hard work was their culture, as was taking care of each other and celebrating their bounty with food and grand occasion. Sharing whatever they had with whoever might show up at dinnertime typified their spirit. Crawfish étouffée and duck and andouille gumbo can be stretched for eight or twelve people.

Our philosophies of life haven't changed much since then. Hurricanes Katrina and Rita did not lessen our desire to live life to the fullest—just the opposite. We lost over 200,000 homes, and of course we're not okay. But we march on, one foot in front of the other, gaining strength from the familiar and from those things that make us who we are: survivors and celebrators of life—here today and now. Fishing, hunting, and cooking are a part of who we are and always will be.

Louisiana license plates do not say "Sportsman's Paradise" because of the football team (though lately "after years of torture" the Saints have been thrilling to watch). It's the outdoors—the myriad ways we interact with the land and the sea and all their inhabitants. Tory has caught catfish with his hands and has trailed alligators. The sight of a shrimp boat with massive nets thrust out of the sides at sunset is forever seared in our mind's eye as the picture of our Louisiana's beauty. Louisiana poetry. Ti once pulled up a turtle trap in a Louisiana bayou only to meet a giant

snapping turtle eye to eye. The memories of crabbing all day on piers in Mississippi with Lally and all of our cousins pulling up trap after trap until we had three garbage cans of crabs. Tory grinning through a battle with a giant tuna on the clearest sunniest day on open waters, then having sushi within minutes.

This is a part of our DNA—a steadfast connection to our rich surroundings. So much of this and the shenanigans that always seem to go along with it were captured on film. This book evolved from our popular television show *Off the Menu* on Turner South, featuring Chef Tory, along with sous-chefs and cooks from Commander's Palace, who go out into the wild to hunt and fish and bring back the day's catch to the Commander's Palace kitchen, where they prepare it in new and fun ways. The show was a natural fit for us since most of our kitchen staff spends their free time hunting and fishing. It's really quite astonishing. We've come to believe that the question "Do you hunt or fish?" must be on our job application somewhere.

The book focuses on two topics, about which we are personally passionate: cooking and celebrating the riches of the land and water. We recapture the fun and adventure of hunting deer and alligator, sportfishing for tuna, pulling in crab traps, and all the glorious cooking that happens afterward. We combine the quick one-pot cooking that takes place at camp when you return, ravenous, with your limit of ducks, with the innovative game and fish cooking of Commander's Palace, and we include great recipes for backyard bashes. Essential guidelines on preparing game and fish—whether they be the treasures of the hunter or fisherman or the bounty available in most supermarkets—are provided and interlaced with our wisdom gained from years of experience.

The advice is right-on practical, and we want you to read it, but more importantly, we want you to cook and expand your repertoire of dishes to include game and new-to-you varieties of fish and shellfish. Venison, buffalo, elk, and duck are too darn flavorful to go unnoticed, and they're readily available at markets across the country. An ever-expanding variety of fish and shellfish are transferred from the water to your table quicker and fresher than ever before. Now more than ever, there is no excuse not to leave behind those bland boneless chicken breasts for the exuberant, bold flavors of game and fish. And there is something about these adventures that bring out, let's just say, "the full personality" in all of us. It wouldn't be an early morning hunt without a practical joke or two. Yes, our team and our family work hard and play hard. We like to play in the wild. So here's to your wild side—and ours!

SEA

Saltwater Adventures

THIS IS NOT A BAD GIG AT ALL: Chef Tory goes to Costa Rica in pursuit of world-class sport fishing, an all-expenses-paid trip to Central America, targeting Pacific sailfish and yellowfin tuna. And this is his *job*.

After months of Tory's suggestions, the Turner South gang gave in to his dream fishing trip. The film crew captured a magical moment: two magnificent sailfish splashing and dancing across the water. Ti doesn't know what was better at the time—the powerful, graceful fish or the irrepressible grin on Tory's face.

On the way to and from the sailfish, we passed one school of tuna after another. Tuna live in the same area as sailfish, in 200-foot-deep water. "They smash your line and take off," says Tory, "and the fight is on. You're strapped in the big chair, the sun blazing above you, fighting a tuna and trying not to lose it. It exhausts you, and just when you think it's over, the tuna challenges you again. You finally manage to bring the tuna near the boat. The deckhand, with a gaff hook and gloves, hauls the fish into the boat with one sweeping motion. Everyone runs to the opposite side of the boat to avoid being cut by a forty-pound tuna with super-sharp fins."

"The tuna is heaved into the tuna box, lines are rebaited, and we're fishing again," Ti says. "I look over my shoulder and see the ruby red color of the impeccably fresh tuna. I sit and watch Tory work, and suddenly I have a newfound respect for the tuna."

Shrimp, oysters, lobster, snapper, grouper, and their saltwater kin are gifts from the sea whether you're out on a boat catching them yourself or are buying them at the fish market. Shellfish and fish thrive when they're complemented by similar flavor profiles. For example, flounder is so delicate, it mates perfectly with subtle flavors such as white wine and crab, whereas amberjack begs for assertive Creole seasoning and the grill.

For shellfish and fish to shine with peak flavor, freshness is critical. If you're not bringing home the day's catch, frequent a high-volume seafood market. Shop for whole fish that have shiny skin and clear eyes; steaks and fish fillets should be cut the same day, and shellfish should smell of the sea with no ammonia odor. Request ice to keep your fish or shellfish cold on the ride home, or bring a cooler in your car.

We're constantly amazed by the variety of sea treasures and the numerous ways to prepare them. We want to continue being astonished, so we avoid endangered fish and buy from people who fish with the environment in mind. If you want to make wise choices for your meals, check out www.seafoodwatch.org from the Monterey Bay Aquarium.

TASSO-STUFFED SHRIMP WITH ROASTED GARLIC CREAM

Shrimp, shrimp, shrimp! It's America's favorite seafood, and maybe the world's. There are many different varieties, shapes, and sizes to choose from, but beware: All shrimp are not created equal! It's a little-known fact that more than 85 percent of the shrimp consumed in the United States is imported and farm raised. I find that there is a massive difference in quality between locally caught, wild American shrimp and the imported farm-raised varieties, and today you have a choice.

Wild American shrimp have a firmer and crisper texture, due to living in the tidal waters of the Gulf of Mexico, the Florida Keys, and the Atlantic Ocean. The flavors are sweet and briney and have a remarkably clean and pure flavor that is unmatched by anything else we've tried. By purchasing wild American shrimp, you support local economies and generations of shrimpers who live and work in areas that have been hit hard by hurricanes. From Texas all the way to the Carolinas, we're seeing record catches of this sustainable seafood, with amazing quality. Look for Certified Wild American Shrimp in your local grocery store or fish market. It's a government seal for quality and freshness, much like the beef industry's Prime, Choice, and Select. For me, the choice is clear: Commander's Palace will use only clean, locally caught, wild American shrimp.

• SERVES 4 AS A FIRST COURSE •

GARLIC CREAM

1 head garlic

1 teaspoon Creole seasoning, store-bought or homemade (see box, page 9)

2 cups heavy cream

1 tablespoon vegetable oil

1 tablespoon minced garlic

4 ounces tasso, finely chopped (see box, page 10)

1 leek (white part only), halved lengthwise, sliced, and rinsed well

¼ cup finely diced green bell pepper

¼ cup finely diced red bell pepper

¼ cup finely diced yellow bell pepper

1¼ teaspoons Creole seasoning, store-bought or homemade (see box, page 9)

12 large shrimp, peeled and deveined

Prepare the garlic cream: Preheat the oven to 350°F. Wrap the garlic in aluminum foil and roast it for 35 minutes, until soft. Cut off the stem end of the garlic head and squeeze the cloves into a medium saucepan. Add the Creole seasoning, then mash the garlic with a fork. Add the cream, bring to a low boil, and cook over medium heat until the cream is reduced by half, about 10 minutes. Keep the sauce on very low heat.

Preheat the oven to 400°F. Lightly grease a baking sheet.

Heat the oil in a large skillet over medium-high heat. Add the garlic and sauté for 20 seconds. Add the tasso and sauté until it starts to shrink, about 1 minute. Add the leek, bell peppers, and 1 teaspoon of the Creole seasoning. Sauté until the vegetables are soft, 3 minutes. Let cool.

With a sharp paring knife, butterfly the shrimp from the underside (not the normal vein side). Place 1 tablespoon of the filling along the butterflied underside of each shrimp, and wrap the tail up and over the filling. Season the tops of the shrimp with the remaining ¼ teaspoon Creole seasoning. Place the shrimp on the prepared baking sheet and bake for about 12 minutes, until they are pink and cooked through. Serve the shrimp on plates that have been drizzled with the Garlic Cream.

TORY'S IMPROV

This recipe can be fancy or not. At camp, just stuff the shrimp and forget about the Garlic Cream. If you want to go whole hog for a special dinner at home, serve the shrimp with the outrageous cream and garnish them with a variety of chopped fresh herbs.

CREOLE SEASONING

We sprinkle this appealingly assertive seasoning mixture in small quantities over seafood, shellfish, all sorts of meat, and even vegetables. Actually, there is little food that comes to the table without it. We developed the blend in Commander's kitchen sometime in the 1970s, and it's still mighty good today. It will keep for months in an airtight container in a cool, dark place, so you might as well make a lot of it.

1 cup table salt	¾ cup freshly ground black pepper
¾ cup Spanish paprika	¼ cup dried thyme
¾ cup onion powder	2 tablespoons dried oregano
¾ cup garlic powder	1 tablespoon cayenne pepper, or to taste

Combine all the ingredients in a large bowl and store in an airtight container.

Tasso is a lean cut of brined, smoked, and heavily spiced pork. It's most often seasoned with salt, paprika, and cayenne pepper or some blend of Cajun or Creole seasoning. After brining and smoking, tasso itself is used as a seasoning for Jambalaya, soups, stews, gumbos, and the like. It can be wrapped tightly and refrigerated or frozen for weeks.

Coconut Beer–Battered Shrimp
with Satsuma Marmalade

This dish is really retro and was popular at Commander's Palace in the '80s, but it's still a winner because it brings together everything that makes food exciting to eat: sweet, sour, salty, bitter, and spicy flavors. A vibrant spicy marmalade, made with satsumas and Creole mustard, offsets the richness of the irresistible fried coconut coating. Mark this page now because you'll definitely make this again.

Big shrimp aren't always better, especially in this recipe. If you use large shrimp, the coconut will burn and the shrimp will be raw in the middle. Another note: Fry these at 325°F. It's a lower temperature than normal frying, but it will prevent the coconut from burning too quickly. If you have any marmalade left over, it sasses up everything from grilled pork and duck to venison and grilled shrimp.

• SERVES 4 TO 6 AS A FIRST COURSE •

SATSUMA MARMALADE

8 satsumas or tangerines, peel and pith removed

2 cups light corn syrup

3 tablespoons Creole mustard or other mild whole-grain mustard

2 teaspoons prepared horseradish

Vegetable oil for frying

24 medium shrimp (about 1½ pounds), peeled, deveined, and butterflied with tails left on

6 teaspoons Creole seasoning, store-bought or homemade (see box, page 9), plus additional to taste

One 12-ounce bottle amber or Pilsner beer

1 cup all-purpose flour

1 cup cornstarch

2 cups sweetened coconut flakes

Prepare the satsuma marmalade: Holding a satsuma over a bowl to collect the juices, run a sharp knife alongside the white membranes to remove the segments. Place the segments in a separate bowl. Repeat with the remaining satsumas, collecting the juice and segments separately. Combine the corn syrup, mustard, horseradish, and the reserved juice in a saucepan, and bring to a boil. Reduce the heat slightly and cook at a low boil until very thick, about 25 minutes. Add the segments, remove from the heat, and let cool to room temperature before serving. (The marmalade can be made up to 2 weeks ahead; cover and refrigerate.)

Fill a medium-size saucepan halfway with oil, and heat it to 325°F.

Toss the shrimp with 2 teaspoons of the Creole seasoning. Combine the beer, flour, cornstarch, and remaining 4 teaspoons Creole seasoning in a bowl, and whisk until smooth. Place the coconut in a shallow dish. Holding the shrimp by the tail, coat each shrimp in the beer batter, shake to remove any excess, and then dredge it in the coconut, pressing well so it adheres. Carefully add the shrimp, in batches, to the hot oil and cook, turning once, until golden brown and crisp, about 4 minutes, Drain on paper towels and season with Creole seasoning. Serve the shrimp with the marmalade alongside.

Oyster and Leek Gratin

Oysters and leeks make a dynamic duo, enhanced here with chopped artichoke hearts and fresh herbs. The gratin comes out of the oven bubbling in its juices and with a cheesy, buttery bread-crumb topping. Trust us, you will want to mop up every lush drop with a piece of crusty bread. This dish can function as a first course for a sit-down dinner or be paired with a salad for a satisfying casual dinner. Remember that the salinity of oysters varies, so do not finish seasoning the dish until the oysters have been added to the pan.

• SERVES 4 AS A FIRST COURSE •

4 tablespoons (½ stick) unsalted butter

1 tablespoon minced shallot

1 tablespoon minced garlic

1 leek (white part only), halved lengthwise, sliced thin, and rinsed well (2 cups)

Pinch plus 1 teaspoon kosher salt

Pinch plus ½ teaspoon ground white pepper

1 cup chopped artichoke hearts

¼ cup dry white wine

1 cup oysters (16 to 20), drained, ¼ cup oyster liquor reserved

2 cups heavy cream

½ cup grated Gruyère or Swiss cheese

½ cup fine dry bread crumbs

½ tablespoon chopped fresh thyme

½ tablespoon chopped fresh oregano

½ tablespoon chopped fresh basil

Preheat the oven to 450°F.

Melt the butter in a heavy 12-inch skillet over medium-high heat. Add the shallot and garlic and cook, stirring, for 20 seconds. Add the leek, a pinch each of salt and white pepper, and cook, stirring, for 30 seconds. Add the artichokes and stir to combine. Add the wine and oyster liquor, bring to a boil, and cook, stirring occasionally, until the mixture is thick and the liquid is reduced to about 1 tablespoon, about 3 minutes. Add the cream, bring to a boil, and cook, stirring occasionally, until reduced by half, for 7 to 8 minutes. Remove the skillet from the heat and stir in the oysters.

Combine the cheese, bread crumbs, and herbs in a small bowl. Adjust the seasoning if necessary with the remaining salt and white pepper.

Divide the oyster mixture among four 1-cup ramekins, and top each one with the bread-crumb mixture. Place the ramekins on a baking sheet and bake for about 8 minutes, until bubbly and golden brown on top.

PARMESAN-CRUSTED OYSTER SALAD

A fantastic first course: hot fried oysters embellished with a dusting of Parmesan cheese, sitting on top of crunchy romaine hearts dressed in a zesty anchovy dressing. The anchovies in this recipe are not the canned variety that you'll find on the shelf, but rather the fresh version in the seafood section. We often serve these Parmesan-crusted fried oysters on their own as hors d'oeuvres or add them to po'boys.

• SERVES 4 AS A FIRST COURSE OR LIGHT LUNCH •

ANCHOVY DRESSING

4 white anchovies (available at gourmet markets)

1 large egg

1 small shallot, chopped

¼ cup freshly grated good-quality Parmigiano-Reggiano cheese

2 tablespoons cane or red wine vinegar

1 teaspoon fresh lemon juice

½ teaspoon freshly ground black pepper

½ teaspoon kosher salt

¾ cup canola oil

SALAD

2 romaine hearts, cored and halved lengthwise

Kosher salt and freshly ground black pepper to taste

4 roma (plum) tomatoes, quartered

1 cup assorted pitted olives, chopped

2 large hard-boiled eggs, diced

8 white anchovies

FRIED OYSTERS

Canola oil for frying

1½ cups masa flour (masa harina)

1½ cups all-purpose flour

2 tablespoons Creole seasoning, store-bought or homemade (see box, page 9)

32 shucked oysters (about 1 pint)

¼ cup freshly grated good-quality Parmigiano-Reggiano cheese

Prepare the anchovy dressing: In a blender, combine all the dressing ingredients except the oil, and blend for 30 seconds. With the motor running, gradually add the oil, blending until the dressing is emulsified. (The dressing can be made up to 2 days ahead; cover and refrigerate.)

Prepare the salad: Divide the romaine among four plates, and drizzle a little dressing over and in between the leaves. Season with salt and pepper. In a medium bowl, combine the tomatoes, olives, eggs, and anchovies; drizzle with

1 tablespoon of the dressing, tossing to coat. Divide the mixture over the romaine.

Prepare the oysters: Heat 3 inches of oil in a large pot to 350°F. In a large bowl, combine the two flours with the Creole seasoning. Add the oysters, in batches, to the flour mixture and toss to coat. Be sure the oysters are very dry. Fry the oysters, in four batches, in the hot oil until golden brown and crisp, about 2½ minutes. Be sure to let the oil return to 350°F between batches. Transfer the fried oysters to a large bowl, add the cheese, and toss to coat.

Place the oysters over the salad and drizzle the remaining dressing around the plates.

LOBSTER AND RED BEAN SUCCOTASH

We love succotash—it's Southern comfort food. For superb succotash worthy of a party, we make this version with lobster, little bits of andouille, and fresh tarragon. We like to serve this over Louisiana popcorn rice (see box). For the best lobster cooking method, look to Creole Lobster Bisque (page 168).

• SERVES 4 AS A MAIN COURSE •

1 cup (2 sticks) plus 2 tablespoons
   unsalted butter, diced

1 cup diced onions

½ cup diced andouille sausage

1½ cups lobster stock or canned
   low-sodium chicken broth

1 cup cooked red kidney beans

1 cup cooked white navy beans

1 cup cooked baby lima beans

½ cup sweet corn kernels (smoked if
   possible)

¼ cup cane vinegar

1 teaspoon kosher salt

¼ teaspoon ground white pepper

4 cups chopped cooked lobster meat
   (from about four 1½-pound lobsters)

1 cup diced fresh tomatoes

1 tablespoon minced fresh tarragon

In a large pot over medium heat, combine the 2 tablespoons butter, the onions, and the andouille. Cook for 3 minutes. Add the stock, beans, corn, vinegar, salt, and white pepper, and bring to a simmer. Cook for 10 minutes, stirring occasionally. Add the lobster meat, tomatoes, and tarragon, and return to a simmer. Add the remaining 2 sticks butter, a few pieces at a time, until all the butter is melted and incorporated.

POPCORN RICE

Rice grows all over Louisiana and rounds out many of our meals. Popcorn is a variety of rice with a subtle popcorn aroma and a flavor that is similar to basmati. We get our popcorn rice from a small company in Lake Charles, Louisiana, where it is harvested from nearby fields.

Jamaican Conch Callaloo

Conch diving in the Bahamas is a blast. Put a scuba mask on, hold your breath, and go for it. Conch live in snail-like cone-shaped shells and are shucked to get at the dense, tough meat. There are only two ways to cook conch: We either cook it very quickly over a super-hot grill, then slice it paper-thin like sashimi and squeeze fresh lime juice across the top; or we simmer it for at least 3 hours in a flavorful broth to tenderize the tough meat, let it cool, and then chop it into small pieces for soups, stews, and fritters.

Callaloo is a Jamaican soup made with callaloo, the leaf of the taro plant. The greens are poisonous when raw and can be eaten only when fully cooked. If you can't find callaloo, use spinach, collards, or mustard greens.

One of the reasons Tory loves Caribbean food is because of its interplay of sweet, sour, salt, and spice. These elements can be found in this soup. And of course he loves eating it on the beach in nothing but his swim trunks and sunglasses.

• SERVES 4 •

1 pound conch

2 tablespoons Creole seasoning, store-bought or homemade (see box, page 9)

1 bay leaf

¼ cup vegetable oil

½ cup finely chopped onion

½ cup finely chopped celery

2 tablespoons seeded and minced Scotch bonnet peppers

1 teaspoon kosher salt, plus additional to taste

½ cup diced sweet potato

¼ cup plus 2 teaspoons dark rum

2 cups chicken stock or canned low-sodium chicken broth

One 14-ounce can light unsweetened coconut milk

2 tablespoons fresh lime juice

1 tablespoon sugar, plus additional to taste

2 cups very thinly sliced callaloo or spinach

¼ cup chopped fresh parsley

Combine the conch, Creole seasoning, bay leaf, and 1 gallon of water in a large pot and bring to a boil over medium heat. Reduce the heat to a simmer and cook the conch, uncovered, for 3 hours. Drain the conch in a colander, let it cool, and then chop it fine. (The cooked conch can be frozen for up to 2 months.)

Heat the oil in a medium pot over medium-high heat. Add the onion, celery, Scotch bonnet peppers, and salt, then cook, stirring, until the vegetables start to soften, about 3 minutes. Add the sweet potato and ¼ cup rum, and cook until the rum has evaporated, about 30 seconds. Add the chicken stock, coconut milk, lime juice, and sugar and bring to a simmer. Cook until the sweet potato is tender, 13 to 14 minutes. Add the conch, callaloo, and parsley and cook, stirring occasionally, for 5 minutes. Stir in the remaining 2 teaspoons rum and adjust the seasoning as needed with salt and sugar.

HURRICANE HOLE CONCH FRITTERS

Hurricane holes are found all over the Caribbean—they are essentially the deepest and most well-protected ports in the islands, where people moor their boats during tropical storms and hurricanes. Conch fritter shacks are a feature of all port towns, and this recipe is based on one Tory learned while living in Coral Bay on St. John. Throw on some reggae, make some conch fritters, and you've got a party.

• MAKES 50; SERVES 12 AS AN HORS D'OEUVRE •

Vegetable oil for frying

3 cups all-purpose flour

1 pound cooked conch meat, chopped fine (see page 17)

1 bunch green onions (green part only), sliced

½ cup minced onion

½ cup minced carrot

½ cup minced red bell pepper

2 tablespoons Creole seasoning, store-bought or homemade (see box, page 9), plus additional to taste

1 tablespoon freshly ground black pepper

1 tablespoon chopped fresh thyme

2 teaspoons baking powder

¼ teaspoon kosher salt

Heat 3 inches of oil in a large pot to 350°F.

In a large bowl, stir all the remaining ingredients with 2½ cups water until a thick, pancake-like batter is formed. Let rest for 5 minutes to activate the baking powder.

Using two large soupspoons, scoop the batter with one and with the other, push the batter off the spoon into the oil. Fry the fritters, in batches, until deep golden brown and cooked through, 3½ minutes. Transfer them to paper towels to drain, and season with Creole seasoning.

HERB-ROASTED SNAPPER WITH BROWN BUTTER VINAIGRETTE

Plain old butter can't stand up to the nutty, fragrant flavor of browned butter. In this recipe we take browned butter and make a luscious, thick sauce that has the consistency of hollandaise. It goes great with grilled lobster, shrimp, and whatever else you normally put butter on. In our case, that would be everything!

• SERVES 4 •

BROWN BUTTER VINAIGRETTE

8 tablespoons (1 stick) unsalted butter

1 large egg

Juice of ½ lemon

Pinch of kosher salt

Pinch of ground white pepper

4 sprigs fresh thyme

4 sprigs fresh tarragon

4 sprigs fresh basil

4 sprigs fresh cilantro

Four 6-ounce snapper fillets

Kosher salt and freshly ground black pepper to taste

½ cup dry white wine

Juice of 2 lemons

1 tablespoon unsalted butter, at room temperature

Prepare the brown butter vinaigrette: In a small saucepan, melt the butter over medium-high heat, swirling it occasionally, until the butter is brown, 10 to 12 minutes. Pour the butter into a bowl and let it cool to almost room temperature.

In another small bowl, whisk together the egg, lemon juice, salt, pepper, and 2 tablespoons water. Gradually whisk the melted butter into the egg mixture and continue whisking until thickened and smooth. Set aside at room temperature.

Preheat the oven to 400°F.

Scatter the herb sprigs on a rimmed baking dish. Season the snapper fillets on both sides with salt and pepper, and arrange them on top of the herbs. Pour the wine and lemon juice over the fillets, and rub the tops evenly with the butter. Roast for 15 to 20 minutes, or until the fish is just cooked through. It should be moist, with the edges just starting to turn brown. Serve the fish drizzled with the brown butter vinaigrette, and place the herbs alongside.

WHOLE GRILLED SNAPPER WITH CITRUS, HERBS, AND CHILES

This is get-your-hands-messy cooking. You work a big bowlful of lemons, herbs, and chiles with your hands to release their juices and oils. Then the mixture is poured over the fish and the whole thing, baking sheet and all, is placed on the grill and cooked. This is the best and easiest way we know to grill whole fish without losing some skin and pieces of fish to the fire gods.

A warning: Use rubber gloves when handling chiles in this and any other recipe. Trust us on this one.

• SERVES 4 •

Two 2½- to 3-pound snappers, scaled and cleaned
1 medium poblano pepper, julienned
1 lemon, cut into ¼-inch-thick slices
1 lime, cut into ¼-inch-thick slices
1 orange, cut into ¼-inch-thick slices
1 bunch fresh flat-leaf parsley, chopped
1 bunch fresh cilantro, chopped

3 jalapeño peppers, julienned
2 tablespoons grated fresh ginger
2 tablespoons kosher salt
4 garlic cloves, minced
1 tablespoon freshly ground black pepper
1 teaspoon crushed red pepper flakes
2 tablespoons light brown sugar
¼ cup olive oil

Prepare a medium-hot fire in a grill.

With a sharp knife, score the fish to the bone three times: once right behind the gills, once in the middle, and once toward the tail. Make three more scores along the other side of the fish.

Combine all the ingredients except the fish in a large bowl, and working with your hands, crush the chiles, citrus, and herbs to release their liquids and essential oils. Arrange half of this citrus mixture on a large rimmed baking sheet, and place the fish on top. Stuff more citrus mixture inside the fish and in the slits, and top the fish with the remaining mixture. Place the baking sheet directly on the grill, and cover the grill. Grill the fish for 40 to 50 minutes, or until cooked through.

Push the citrus mixture off the top of the fish. With a fork in each hand, gently pull back the skin and discard it. Again using two forks, gently remove pieces of cooked fish from the top fillet and place them on a platter. Next, grab the tail with your hand and slowly pull up the spine to reveal the bottom fillet; discard the spine. Finally, remove the pieces of the bottom fillet. Serve the fish garnished with the citrus mixture, with any pan juices drizzled on top.

TORY'S FISH COOKING TIP

To see if the fish is done, insert a toothpick into the thickest part of the fillet near the spine. If the toothpick passes through easily, then the fish is done.

PRESENTING WHOLE COOKED FISH

At home we like to put the whole fish in the middle of the table and just chow down—no fancy filleting necessary. But if you're cooking for friends, we suggest filleting it this way: First, with a fork in each hand, gently pull back the skin and discard it. Again using two forks, gently remove pieces of cooked fish from the top fillet. Next, grab the tail with your hand and slowly pull up the spine to reveal the bottom fillet; discard the spine. Finally, remove the pieces of the bottom fillet.

CREOLE POACHED GROUPER

If you're in the mood to eat light but not sacrifice flavor, then this recipe is absolutely for you! The grouper and vegetables are poached in crab boil for maximum flavor, and then the poaching liquid is made into a vinaigrette. This recipe takes a simple backyard seafood boil to the next level and is a crowd-pleaser. If you don't have seafood stock, plain old water will be just fine, but not as flavorful.

• SERVES 4 •

POACHING LIQUID

1 quart seafood stock or water

2 medium lemons, halved

1 cup dry white wine

6 large garlic cloves, crushed

3 tablespoons Tabasco sauce

1 tablespoon Creole seasoning, store-bought or homemade (see box, page 9)

2 teaspoons kosher salt

1 teaspoon freshly ground black pepper

2 bay leaves

Four 6- to 8-ounce grouper fillets

2 teaspoons Creole seasoning, store-bought or homemade (see box, page 9)

2 celery stalks, cut into ¼ × 3-inch pieces

2 medium carrots, cut into ¼ × 3-inch pieces

1 large parsnip, cut into ¼ × 3-inch pieces

1 medium onion, cut into ¼ × 3-inch pieces

Juice of 2 lemons

1 teaspoon chopped fresh tarragon

2 tablespoons extra virgin olive oil

Pinch of kosher salt

Pinch of freshly ground black pepper

4 ounces red-leaf lettuce, separated into leaves

Prepare the poaching liquid: Pour the stock into a large pot or Dutch oven. Squeeze the lemon juice into the stock, add all the remaining ingredients, and bring to a boil over high heat. Reduce the heat to medium and simmer, uncovered, for 5 minutes.

Season the grouper fillets on both sides with the Creole seasoning. Carefully add the fish and vegetables to the poaching liquid. Reduce the heat to medium-low and cook, uncovered, until the fish is just cooked through, 10 minutes. Transfer the fish and vegetables to a plate and cover to keep warm.

In a small bowl, combine 3 tablespoons of the warm poaching liquid with lemon juice and the tarragon. Whisk in the oil and season with a pinch each of salt and pepper.

To serve, arrange the lettuce on plates and top with the vegetables. Arrange the fish next to the vegetables, and drizzle the vinaigrette over all.

GRILLED COBIA WITH SHRIMP AND MANGO SALSA

Cobia is at its best when grilled. Its meatiness and oiliness stand up to grilling much better than most other fish—you get the smoky grill flavor without overwhelming the fish. And the refreshing shrimp and mango salsa is a terrific counterpart.

• SERVES 4 •

SHRIMP AND MANGO SALSA

8 ounces whole medium shrimp, peeled, deveined, and cooked

¼ teaspoon cayenne pepper

1 large mango, peeled, seeded, and diced

½ red onion, diced

½ cup diced red bell pepper

Juice of 2 limes

3 tablespoons olive oil

2 tablespoons sugar

2 tablespoons minced fresh cilantro

Kosher salt and freshly ground black pepper to taste

2 teaspoons vegetable oil

Four 6- to 8-ounce cobia fillets

1 tablespoon Creole seasoning, store-bought or homemade (see box, page 9)

Prepare the shrimp and mango salsa: Combine all the ingredients in a large bowl and stir well. Cover and chill for at least 2 hours or up to 2 days ahead.

Prepare a medium-hot fire in a grill.

Drizzle the oil over the fish and rub it in. Sprinkle the Creole seasoning over the fish and pat so it adheres. Grill the fish until the edges begin to turn white, 5 minutes. Turn the fillets over and cook until just cooked through but still springy and soft to the touch, another 5 to 6 minutes. Serve the fish topped with the salsa.

IS THERE A FISHERMAN IN THE HOUSE?

Cobia can weigh over 100 pounds and are very strong and exciting to catch. We fish for them in shallow water, 10 to 50 feet deep, only 100 yards offshore at Destin, Florida, with Tory's buddy and fishing guide Pat Dineen. This is some of the finest fishing that I've ever done, so book a trip today! What are you waiting for?

No cobia? Substitute wahoo, mahimahi, kingfish, or barracuda.

POTATO-CRUSTED SHEEPSHEAD WITH SMOKED TOMATO BUTTER

Crisp, earthy potatoes crust this fish, and a butter sauce with a hint of smoke and zip lends richness. Smoked tomatoes may sound "cheffy," but they're really easy to make and they keep in the refrigerator for a while. They can be added to sandwiches, vegetable sautés, and mayonnaise, pureed into salad dressings, and served alongside steak.

• SERVES 4 •

SMOKED TOMATO BUTTER

2 cups dry white wine

1 cup heavy cream

½ cup coarsely chopped shallots

1 medium lemon, peel and pith removed, coarsely chopped

1 smoked tomato, 2 halves (see box, page 27), diced

10 whole black peppercorns

¼ teaspoon kosher salt, plus additional to taste

⅛ teaspoon ground white pepper, plus additional to taste

12 tablespoons (1½ sticks) cold unsalted butter, cut into pieces

Two 12- to 16-ounce russet potatoes

Four 6- to 8-ounce sheepshead fillets

2½ teaspoons Creole seasoning, store-bought or homemade (see box, page 9)

½ cup all-purpose flour

½ cup milk

2 large eggs

1 cup vegetable oil

Prepare the smoked tomato butter: Combine all the ingredients except the butter in a medium saucepan and bring to a simmer over medium heat. Simmer until reduced by three quarters, 25 to 30 minutes. Remove the saucepan from the heat and add the butter, several pieces at a time, whisking constantly until all the butter is incorporated and an emulsion is formed. Adjust the seasoning with salt and pepper. Strain the sauce through a fine-mesh strainer into another pan, pressing against the solids with the back of a spoon. Keep it warm on the back of the stove; the sauce should be just at body temperature.

Preheat the oven to 350°F.

Julienne the potatoes, using a mandoline if you have one or a knife. Place the julienned potatoes in a large bowl and stir well with your hands while rinsing under cold running water for about 20 minutes, until the water runs clear. Drain well and pat dry with paper towels.

Season both sides of the fish with 2 teaspoons of the Creole seasoning. Combine the flour and remaining ½ teaspoon Creole seasoning in a shallow dish. Whisk the milk and eggs together in a medium bowl. One fillet at a time, dip the fish in the egg wash, let the excess liquid drip off, and then dredge it in the seasoned flour to coat.

Using half of the shredded potatoes, make four piles on a baking sheet and pat each pile into the same size and shape as a fish fillet. Lay the fillets on the potatoes and top with the remaining half of the potatoes, pressing firmly so the potatoes adhere to the fish.

Heat the oil in a 12-inch skillet over medium heat until it is hot but not smoking. Add 2 fish fillets and cook, undisturbed, until the potatoes are brown and crisp, 5 to 6 minutes. With a metal spatula, carefully turn the fillets over and cook until the fish is cooked through and the crust is golden brown, another 5 to 6 minutes. Keep the fillets warm while you repeat with the remaining 2 fillets. Serve the fish over pools of the smoked tomato butter.

UGLY FISH

Sheepshead got their name because their face and teeth resemble the bucktoothed face of real sheep. This mild, flaky fish lives in the Gulf of Mexico and is great eating. Sheepshead love to eat crustaceans, and their flavor reflects this diet, strongly resembling crabmeat.

SMOKED TOMATOES

Cut tomatoes in half crosswise and season the cut sides with olive oil, salt, and pepper to taste. When the coals are low (after you've cooked your dinner), set them on the grill, cut sides up. Cover the coals with fresh wood chips, close the grill, and let the tomatoes cook for about 20 minutes. The tomatoes will absorb the smoky flavor of the closed grill and stay juicy to boot.

Morel-Dusted Sheepshead with Pinot Noir Reduction

Sheepshead, or bay snapper, can be caught several different ways. Most commonly, trotlines are baited with broken blue crab legs and circle hooks stretched evenly 5 to 10 feet apart, and sunk directly onto the bottom of the water. You can also catch them with a rod and reel off the beach in the Gulf of Mexico, or in a deep cut or channel where the water flows quickly, or even near the pilings under a trestle in slower-moving water.

Dried mushrooms need only a few seconds of buzzing in a spice grinder to make a quick and zesty crust for the fish. Any extra morel dust can be sprinkled on chicken, steaks, and cream sauces for pasta.

• SERVES 4 •

PINOT NOIR REDUCTION

1½ cups Pinot Noir

½ cup light corn syrup

1 bay leaf

½ teaspoon kosher salt, plus additional to taste

¼ teaspoon freshly ground black pepper, plus additional to taste

3 tablespoons cold unsalted butter, cut into pieces

1 ounce dried morel mushrooms

Four 6- to 8-ounce skinless sheepshead fillets

½ teaspoon kosher salt

¼ teaspoon ground white pepper

2 tablespoons vegetable oil

2 tablespoons unsalted butter

Prepare the Pinot Noir reduction: Place the wine, corn syrup, bay leaf, salt, and pepper in a medium saucepan and bring to a simmer over medium heat. Simmer until reduced to about 3 tablespoons, about 15 minutes. Remove from the heat and add the butter, several pieces at a time, whisking constantly until the sauce is smooth. Taste, and adjust the seasoning. Remove the bay leaf and set the pan aside on the stove to keep warm.

Grind the mushrooms to a fine powder in a spice grinder. Season both sides of the fish with the salt and white pepper. Then sprinkle ¼ teaspoon of the morel dust on each side; pat it into the fish to coat evenly.

In a large nonstick skillet, heat 1 tablespoon of the oil and 1 tablespoon of the butter over medium-high heat until the butter foams. Add 2 fillets, presentation side down, and sear until golden brown, about 3 minutes. Turn the fish over and cook for 2 minutes, until just cooked through. Keep the fillets warm while you repeat with the remaining 2 fillets. Serve the fish drizzled with the wine sauce.

No sheepshead? Substitute trout, flounder, or any other delicate fish.

CLEANING A COFFEE GRINDER

Coffee grinders are ideal for grinding spices, but you need to clean them thoroughly between uses so the spice flavors don't linger. We've found that a paper towel just doesn't cut it, but rice does the trick every time. Simply grind uncooked rice in the coffee grinder right after you grind spices—the rice picks up any leftover bits and fragrance.

PECAN BUTTER–BASTED FLOUNDER
WITH CREOLE MUSTARD CREAM

There is flaky moist fish and nutty butter in every bite of this dish. At Commander's Palace,
we serve asparagus alongside for color and add a dollop of American caviar over the fish.
Make extra pecan butter because it's great on toast, pancakes, and even vegetables.
Flounder is very mild in flavor, so we use seasoning sparingly.

• SERVES 4 •

PECAN BUTTER

6 tablespoons (¾ stick) cold unsalted
  butter, coarsely chopped

½ cup pecan pieces

Pinch of kosher salt

Pinch of freshly ground black pepper

CREOLE MUSTARD CREAM

1 cup heavy cream

¼ cup dry white wine

Juice of 1 lemon

2 tablespoons minced shallot

1 tablespoon Creole mustard

Pinch of kosher salt

Pinch of freshly ground black pepper

2 tablespoons cold unsalted butter, cut
  into pieces

Eight 4-ounce flounder fillets

2 teaspoons Creole seasoning,
  store-bought or homemade
  (see box, page 9)

1 teaspoon chopped fresh chives

Prepare the pecan butter: Combine all the ingredients in the bowl of a food processor and process for about 40 seconds, until smooth.

Prepare the Creole mustard cream: Place the cream, wine, lemon juice, shallot, mustard, salt, and pepper in a small saucepan and bring to a simmer over
medium heat. Simmer until reduced by half, about 12 minutes. Remove from the
heat and whisk in the butter, several pieces at a time, whisking constantly to form
an emulsion. Adjust the seasoning to taste and keep warm.

Preheat the oven to 450°F.

Season both sides of the fillets with the Creole seasoning and arrange them,
presentation side down, on a cutting board. Place 1 tablespoon of the pecan butter on each fillet and spread it out evenly, covering the whole fillet. Starting with
the flat tail portion, roll each fillet up to form a cylinder. Stand the rolls upright

on a baking sheet. (Make sure the rolls are stable by placing the heavier side of the roll directly on the baking sheet.)

Place ½ tablespoon of the remaining pecan butter on the top of each roll, and spread it out with the back of a spoon so that as the fish bake, the butter will run down inside the roll. Bake for 16 to 17 minutes, until the fish is cooked through and tender and a toothpick passes easily through the center.

Place the flounder "tournedos" on a serving platter or on individual plates, drizzle with the Creole mustard cream, and garnish with the chives.

CRISPY POMPANO WITH SPICY CAYENNE BUTTER

Pompano has been a New Orleans favorite for years, as it comes right out of the Gulf of Mexico. You can grill or pan-fry it, but either way, we always leave the skin on because it contributes flavor. A Creole-inspired spiced butter makes pompano even juicier than usual; all you have to do is soften the butter and mix in the spices and parsley.

• SERVES 4 •

SPICY CAYENNE BUTTER

Juice of 1 lemon

1½ teaspoons cayenne pepper

½ teaspoon cracked black peppercorns

1 teaspoon kosher salt

1 teaspoon sugar

1 tablespoon chopped fresh parsley

4 tablespoons (½ stick) unsalted butter, at room temperature

Four 6- to 7-ounce pompano fillets, skin on

2 teaspoons Creole seasoning, store-bought or homemade (see box, page 9), plus additional to taste

½ cup all-purpose flour

½ cup cornstarch

2 tablespoons vegetable oil

Prepare the spicy cayenne butter: In a small bowl, stir together the lemon juice, cayenne pepper, black pepper, salt, sugar, and parsley until the spices absorb the lemon juice and a loose paste is formed. Add the butter and stir until the mixture is smooth and pink in color. The seasoning in the butter will intensify the longer it sits, so wait at least 5 minutes before serving. (The butter can be prepared up to 7 days ahead and refrigerated, or frozen for up to 1 month.)

THE CRISP IS ON

To get the crispest skin possible, cornstarch mixed with flour is our coating of choice—it comes out crisper than flour alone. Cornstarch is the secret ingredient of tempura, used for its lightness and crisping abilities.

Season the fish on both sides with the Creole seasoning. Sprinkle the flour and cornstarch evenly across a baking sheet, or mix with a fork and then use your fingertips to combine. Lay the pompano fillets on the cornstarch mixture, skin side down, and let them sit for 4 minutes.

Add the oil to a large skillet and heat over medium-high heat for 3 minutes, until hot but not smoking. Pick up the fillets, shaking them to remove excess cornstarch mixture. Lay the fillets in the skillet, skin side down, and gently shake to prevent sticking. Cook for 3½ to 4 minutes, until each fillet is crisp and browned evenly across the bottom. Gently turn the fish over and cook for 1 minute more.

Spoon the cayenne butter over the fish, allow it to melt, and then serve.

CAREFUL! HOT OIL SPLASHES

When adding fish fillets to hot oil, always drape the fillets into the pan from front to back. This ensures that any splashes of hot oil will head towards the back of the pan and not on you. We've learned this the hard way, but had to learn it only once.

GRILLED POMPANO WITH ORANGE CARAMEL GLAZE

Sharp and citrusy with a buttery caramel finish, this sauce is unbelievable with pompano. It also matches up nicely with many other types of seafood, especially scallops. The sauce involves a degree of fuss, but it is easy relative to its power to knock your socks off. Be sure not to have the heat too high—you don't want to ruin your caramel by scorching it.

• SERVES 4 •

ORANGE CARAMEL GLAZE

2 cups fresh orange juice

2 medium shallots, chopped

1 tablespoon sugar

1 bay leaf

¼ cup heavy cream

8 tablespoons (1 stick)
    unsalted butter

Pinch of kosher salt

Pinch of ground white pepper

1 tablespoon vegetable oil

Four 6- to 7-ounce pompano fillets

2 teaspoons Creole seasoning,
    store-bought or homemade
    (see box, page 9)

Prepare the orange caramel glaze: Combine the orange juice, shallots, sugar, and bay leaf in a medium saucepan and bring to a simmer over medium heat. Cook, stirring constantly with a heat-resistant silicone spatula, until the mixture is thick, a rich dark caramel has formed, and a nutty aroma has developed, 15 to 20 minutes. It is very, very important that as the caramel starts to form, you do not leave the stove, or it will burn and you will have to start over.

Add the cream slowly—it will immediately boil vigorously. Continue stirring with the spatula. After the cream is well incorporated, remove the pan from the heat. Cool for 5 minutes. Then whisk in the butter until melted. Discard the bay leaf, and season with the salt and white pepper.

Prepare a medium-hot fire in a grill.

Drizzle the oil over the fish and rub it in. Season both sides of the fish with the Creole seasoning. When the grill is hot, spray the rack with vegetable oil spray. Place the fish pointing toward the 2 o'clock position and cook for 2 minutes. Using a fish spatula, gently pull up fillets and rotate them to the 10 o'clock position; cook for 2 minutes. Gently turn the fillets over and cook until cooked through, 2 to 3 minutes more. Serve the pompano drizzled with the orange caramel glaze.

TORY'S TIP

When reducing the orange juice mixture in this recipe, don't let it caramelize and scorch around the inside rim of the saucepan or it will become bitter and dark in color.

BEAUTIFUL GRILL MARKS

Start out with an even-burning grill—the left and right sides should be the same temperature. Take the preheated grill rack and brush on an ample amount of vegetable oil by wadding up a kitchen towel, dipping it in oil, and rubbing it on the rack from back to front. Or you can simply spray the rack with vegetable oil spray. Place whatever you're grilling pointing toward the 2 o'clock position and let it hang out there to get a nice sear. Then, using a fish spatula or tongs for steaks, gently pull up the fillet and rotate it to the 10 o'clock position to get the desired crosshatch pattern. Finally, flip the food over and cook on the other side to finish grilling.

Grilled Wahoo and Pineapple Salad with Lime Ginger Vinaigrette

Wahoo is the fastest fish in the ocean and a blast to catch. They're a big ball of angry muscle with razor-sharp teeth, and will put up a great fight. For all the fishermen out there, you know what we mean when we say you better have your heavy steel leader. Wahoo tend to live in the same waters as mahimahi, kingfish, and barracuda, so you usually catch one alongside the others.

Wahoo are very lean (all that fast swimming means very little fat), so don't overcook them—it takes only a couple of minutes on each side, depending on the thickness of the steaks, to get them to the desired medium to medium-well doneness. This bright salad will transport you to sunnier shores.

• SERVES 4 •

Lime Ginger Vinaigrette

½ cup fresh lime juice, preferably from Key limes

2 tablespoons finely grated fresh ginger

2 tablespoons sugar

Pinch of kosher salt

Pinch of freshly ground black pepper

Pinch of crushed red pepper flakes

1½ cups vegetable oil

1 tablespoon vegetable oil

Four 6-ounce wahoo steaks (about ¾ inch thick)

1 tablespoon Creole seasoning, store-bought or homemade (see box, page 9)

½ pineapple, peeled, trimmed, and cut into ½-inch-thick rings

1 red bell pepper

8 cups salad greens

1 large avocado, cut into long, thin slices

½ small red onion, sliced very thin and rinsed

Kosher salt and freshly ground black pepper to taste

Prepare a medium-hot fire in a grill.

Prepare the lime ginger vinaigrette: Combine all the ingredients except the oil in a blender and process for 30 seconds. With the motor running, gradually add the oil and blend until the dressing is emulsified. Set it aside.

Rub the vegetable oil into the wahoo and season both sides with the Creole seasoning. Place the wahoo, pineapple, and the bell pepper on the grill to cook. Cook for 3½ to 4 minutes on each side or until the wahoo is mid-well, the pineapple is tender, and the bell pepper is soft and cooked through. Transfer the fish, pineapple, and bell pepper to a platter.

Peel, seed, and slice the bell pepper into thin strips. Transfer the strips to a large bowl and add the salad greens, avocado, and onion. Season with salt and pepper, and add 2 tablespoons of the vinaigrette, tossing to coat.

To serve, arrange the grilled pineapple on individual plates and top with the lettuce mixture and the grilled fish. Drizzle the remaining vinaigrette over the fish and around the salad.

IS THERE A FISHERMAN IN THE HOUSE?

When butchering wahoo, cut the steaks thin. Thick steaks will dry out too much on the outside while the inside will be rare.

Jamaican Jerk Mahimahi

Tory loves the Caribbean—the intense, spicy foods, the laid-back lifestyle, and the beach. Some of the happiest times of his life have been spent hanging out in wet swim trunks, eating island barbecue, and drinkin' Red Stripe beer. He'd much rather eat at the little roadside huts and jerk shacks than sit down in a fancy restaurant. It's pretty cool to see four generations at work at these casual spots, cooking family recipes with fresh local ingredients straight from their own farms.

Just like American barbecue, jerk has many different styles, but basically jerk is island barbecue: Meat or fish is marinated or heavily seasoned with a dry rub and cooked low and slow over an outside grill. Mahimahi is a perfect choice for jerk because it's meaty and dense, so it can hang out on the grill for a while without overcooking, and then get jerked off the grill and put on the dinner table.

• SERVES 4 •

Dry Jerk Rub

2 teaspoons freshly ground black pepper

2 teaspoons Spanish paprika

1 teaspoon curry powder

1 teaspoon kosher salt

1 teaspoon sugar

1 teaspoon garlic powder

1 teaspoon onion powder

½ teaspoon ground cinnamon

¼ teaspoon ground nutmeg

¼ teaspoon cayenne pepper

Wet Jerk Rub

3 onions, coarsely chopped

2 large tomatoes, coarsely chopped

2 bunches green onions (green part only), chopped

8 large garlic cloves

2 tablespoons chopped fresh thyme

2 tablespoons Tabasco sauce

1 teaspoon kosher salt

½ teaspoon ground allspice

¼ teaspoon ground cloves

Four 6- to 8-ounce mahimahi fillets

Prepare the dry jerk rub: Combine all the ingredients in a small bowl.

Prepare the wet jerk rub: In a food processor, combine all the ingredients and process until smooth.

Season the fish on both sides with the dry rub. Place the fillets in a nonreactive bowl or baking dish and cover with the wet jerk rub. Cover the dish with plastic wrap while you marinate the fish in the refrigerator for at least 1 hour and up to 24 hours.

Prepare the grill: If you're grilling on a gas grill, add presoaked wood chips to the grate and keep the flame on medium-low. If you're grilling with charcoal, let the coals burn until they're covered with white ash and the heat is medium-low.

Remove the fish from the marinade and place directly on the grill. Cook until the edges start to turn white, about 9 minutes, depending on the heat of the grill. Turn the fish over and cook until just cooked through but still springy and soft to the touch, about 10 minutes more.

No mahimahi? Substitute cobia or other dense whitefish fillets.

TORY IMPROV

Jerk can be done with just about every cut of pork, beef, chicken, fish, or goat—and everyone loves a tasty goat, you know.

TORY'S FAVORITE FISH TACOS

Tory came back from his trip to Costa Rica addicted to fish tacos. Now he makes them at home all the time, varying the fish and the crunchy vegetable garnishes. Tory prefers flour tortillas for their texture and flavor, but you can use the more traditional corn ones.

• SERVES 4 AS A MAIN COURSE, OR 8 AS A FIRST COURSE •

Vegetable oil for frying

2 cups all-purpose flour

1 tablespoon Creole seasoning, store-bought or homemade (see box, page 9), plus additional to taste

1 teaspoon baking powder

1 bottle cold Corona beer

1 pound mahimahi fillets, cut into ½ × 3-inch strips

Eight 8-inch flour tortillas, warmed

1½ cups Creole Tartar Sauce (page 151)

1 cup thinly shaved red cabbage (the thinner the better)

2 tomatoes, seeded and cut into strips

1 bunch fresh cilantro, chopped

4 limes, halved

Heat 3 inches of oil in a large pot to 350°F.

In a bowl combine the flour, Creole seasoning, and baking powder. Whisk in the beer until combined and smooth.

In batches, dredge the fish through the batter, let any excess drip off, and then carefully drop into the hot oil. Fry until the fish is golden brown and just cooked through, 3 minutes. Be sure to let the oil return to 350°F between batches. Drain on paper towels.

Arrange the tortillas on a work surface and slather them with the Creole Tartar Sauce. Top with the fish, cabbage, tomatoes, and cilantro. Squeeze the limes over the tacos, and roll up.

No mahimahi? Substitute rare tuna steaks, preferably blackened, sliced thin.

New Orleans Barbecued Amberjack

One of the greatest things about saltwater fishing in the Gulf of Mexico is that you never know how many different species of fish you'll catch in a day. It's not uncommon to hook large grouper, amberjack, cobia, and many different species of snapper.

Amberjack are large fish that will bend your thick saltwater rod and keep it bent for 30 minutes. At the first sign of danger, they know to dart back into safety with the force of a submarine. The trick here is to keep your fish out of the legs and steel tangle of offshore oil rigs.

Amberjack are full-flavored, so they'll stand up to grilling, smoking, blackening, roasting, or our favorite, garlicky New Orleans–style barbecue. Barbecue in New Orleans is not thrown on the grill and slathered with sauce; rather it usually refers to oysters or shrimp sautéed in butter with a ton of garlic and other seasonings. At Commander's Palace, we serve this dish as a main course with white rice, or as an appetizer with a black pepper buttermilk biscuit.

The secret to this dish's success is toasting the garlic to a deep golden brown before adding the other ingredients. This helps to bring out the body in the sauce and delivers more depth and elegance.

• SERVES 4 •

Four 6- to 8-ounce amberjack fillets, sliced thin to increase surface area

2 teaspoons Creole seasoning, store-bought or homemade (see box, page 9)

4 tablespoons (½ stick) cold unsalted butter, cut into pieces

2 tablespoons minced garlic

1 tablespoon minced fresh rosemary

¼ teaspoon freshly ground black pepper

½ cup Abita Amber, or other amber or lager beer

2 tablespoons fresh lemon juice

2 tablespoons Worcestershire sauce

2 tablespoons Tabasco sauce, or to taste

Heat a heavy 12-inch skillet over medium-high heat for 3 minutes.

Season the fish on all sides with the Creole seasoning. Add 2 tablespoons of the butter to the hot skillet. When it has melted, add 2 fillets and lightly shake back and forth for 5 seconds so they don't stick to the bottom of the skillet. Cook until the fish is white around the edges and deep golden brown on the bottom, about 2½ minutes. Turn the fish over and continue to cook until cooked through, 1 more minute. Transfer to a plate and keep warm. Repeat with the remaining fillets.

In the same skillet, cook the garlic over medium heat, stirring constantly and scraping up any bits, until deep golden brown, about 1 minute. Add the rosemary and black pepper and cook, stirring, until fragrant, about 15 seconds. Deglaze the skillet with the beer, lemon juice, Worcestershire, and Tabasco. Cook, stirring constantly, until reduced by half.

Remove the skillet from the heat and whisk in the remaining 2 tablespoons of butter, a few pieces at a time, until all the butter has melted and the sauce is smooth and shiny. Taste, and adjust the seasoning if necessary. Add the fish to the skillet and cook over low heat, basting constantly, until the fillets are warmed through, about 2 minutes.

TORY'S TIP

When you're cooking fish, you don't want to leave the stove, because there's nothing worse than overcooked fish. And fish is less forgiving than, say, steaks on the grill. By the way, amberjack is a dense fish that needs to be cooked all the way through (not like tuna or salmon).

No amberjack? Substitute another meaty fish such as swordfish, kingfish, Spanish mackerel, cobia, or wahoo.

COSTA RICAN TUNA POKE

Costa Rica is one of the best places to go sport fishing because the water is so pristine and because they have strict catch-and-release practices. The fish in these waters are huge, unpredictable, fast, and strong. Most people go bill fishing for marlin and sailfish and catch tuna along the way. Tuna is a lagniappe there, and when we went, there were so many that we couldn't keep them off our lines. Pound for pound there is not a fish out there that swims harder and puts up a better fight than the tuna.

We make this marinade before going tuna fishing, but if we've run out of time, we'll stuff wasabi and packs of soy sauce in our shorts' pockets before we head out.

• SERVES 6 TO 8 •

10 ounces sushi-grade tuna loin, cut into ¼-inch cubes

1 large shallot, minced

1 tablespoon minced fresh ginger

1½ tablespoons soy sauce

1 tablespoon chopped fresh chives

1 teaspoon fresh lemon juice

1 teaspoon fresh lime juice

¾ teaspoon finely grated lemon zest

½ teaspoon sesame oil

½ teaspoon chile oil

¼ teaspoon kosher salt

⅛ teaspoon freshly ground black pepper

1 teaspoon black and/or white sesame seeds

Crackers, for serving

Using a rubber spatula, combine all the ingredients except the sesame seeds in a medium bowl. Stir well, and sprinkle with the sesame seeds. Set the bowl in a larger bowl of ice, to keep the poke cold, and serve crackers alongside.

Blackened Tuna Steaks with Citrus Jalapeño–Spiked Cabbage

This family recipe from our friends Chris and Lisa Barbato is so darn good that we crave it. The cabbage is addictive—and wonderful with backyard barbecue as well as tacos and burritos.

• SERVES 4 •

Citrus Jalapeño–Spiked Cabbage

1 small head white cabbage, shredded fine

3 avocados, diced

2 medium tomatoes, diced

1 small white onion, minced

½ bunch fresh cilantro, chopped

2 jalapeño peppers, seeded and minced

Juice of 2 lemons

Juice of 2 limes

5 garlic cloves, minced

3 tablespoons kosher salt

2 tablespoons freshly ground black pepper

Four 6-ounce yellowfin tuna fillets

1 tablespoon Creole seasoning, store-bought or homemade (see box, page 9)

1 tablespoon vegetable oil

Prepare the citrus jalapeño–spiked cabbage: Combine all the ingredients in a large bowl and toss very well with your hands or two kitchen spoons. Chill, covered, for at least 1 hour and up to 24.

Place the tuna fillets on a kitchen towel and pat very dry. Season them on all sides with the Creole seasoning.

Add the oil to a large heavy skillet and place over high heat for 3 minutes, until hot and almost smoking. Arrange the tuna in the skillet, leaving space between the fillets. Cook for 1½ minutes on each side for rare, 2 minutes for medium-rare. Serve the tuna alongside the cabbage.

Tory's Tip

Always buy the thickest tuna steaks available. Thick steaks will allow you to get a nice sear on the crust while keeping the interior juicy, red, and medium-rare.

BLACKENING 101

Okay, so it may be too '80s for you, but the beauty of blackening when it's done properly (not scorched) is a nice, highly seasoned sear or crust that stands up and pairs well with full-flavored fish or game. The critical components are a scorching-hot pan, preferably cast iron, and super-dry meat. Use a kitchen towel to dry the meat; we find paper towels will stick. One more point: Leave enough space in between the steaks so the meat will sear and not steam.

SEARED SHARK WITH CRUSHED PARSLEY SAUCE

Fishing for shark is so thrilling because of the imminent danger involved. It's a guy thing. You had better be prepared to deal with this large animal if you get one too close to the boat. Have a solid game plan in place concerning everyone's role in bringing this beast aboard. There is little room for error. Needless to say, the fish box had better be open because you don't want a loose live shark thrashing about on deck.

Big fish like shark demand big flavors. We achieve this by seasoning it heavily with Creole seasoning and searing it in a cast-iron skillet. The skillet distributes heat evenly and sears the fish to a deep, rich, golden brown on the outside without burning it. The flavors here meld wonderfully with Fennel Ragout (page 199).

• SERVES 4 •

CRUSHED PARSLEY SAUCE

1½ tablespoons vegetable oil

½ cup fresh parsley leaves (no stems)

Kosher salt and freshly ground black pepper to taste

¼ cup crushed ice

¼ cup olive oil

Four 6- to 8-ounce shark fillets

2 teaspoons Creole seasoning, store-bought or homemade (see box, page 9)

2 tablespoons vegetable oil

Create an ice bath by placing ice and water in a medium bowl. Set a small bowl, wiped dry inside, in the medium bowl.

Prepare the crushed parsley sauce: Heat a medium skillet over high heat for 3 minutes. Add the vegetable oil and swirl until it smokes. Add the parsley, season with salt and pepper, and cook, stirring, until the parsley is wilted but the color is still bright green, 15 seconds. Spoon the parsley into the cold bowl and continue stirring for 2 minutes to cool it. Transfer the parsley, still in the ice bath, to the refrigerator and chill for 15 minutes, until cooled completely.

Transfer the cooled parsley, crushed ice, and 3 tablespoons ice water to a blender and pulse, scraping down the sides as needed, until the mixture comes together, about 2 minutes. With the motor running, add the oil in a stream and process until emulsified, 45 seconds to 1 minute.

Season both sides of the fish with the Creole seasoning. Heat 2 tablespoons of the oil in a large cast-iron skillet over medium-high heat until hot but not smoking. Add the fillets and sear until golden brown, about 3 minutes. Turn the fish over, lower the heat to medium, and sear on the second side until the fish is browned and cooked through, 3 minutes. Serve the shark drizzled with the parsley sauce.

No shark? Substitute any meaty-textured fish, such as swordfish or mahimahi.

Grilled Mako Shark Salad

We love the meaty flavor of shark—the trick is that it must be obtained fresh from a reputable seafood market. Mako is our favorite; it has the mildest flavor of all the shark varieties. If you are unable to find mako, look for other species that have a rosy pink color (similar to veal) and fresh ocean aroma. If shark has an ammonia-like smell, but you know it's fresh and has been properly handled, soak it in milk for a few hours before cooking to remove the scent.

• SERVES 4 •

VINAIGRETTE

1 tablespoon champagne vinegar or cane vinegar

1 tablespoon minced red or yellow bell pepper

Kosher salt and freshly ground black pepper to taste

Pinch of sugar

1/3 cup extra virgin olive oil

Four 6- to 8-ounce mako fillets, or other shark or mahimahi fillets, about 3/4 inch thick

2 1/8 teaspoons Creole seasoning, store-bought or homemade (see box, page 9)

4 ounces mesclun or assorted baby lettuces (about 4 cups)

1 avocado, diced

1 large tomato, sliced thin

2 ounces grape tomatoes, cut in half crosswise (about 1/3 cup)

1 shallot, sliced thin

1/4 cup cane vinegar

1/4 teaspoon kosher salt

1/4 teaspoon freshly ground black pepper

Prepare a medium-hot fire in a grill.

Prepare the vinaigrette: In a small bowl, whisk the vinegar, bell pepper, salt, pepper, and sugar together. Add the oil in a stream, whisking until emulsified. (The vinaigrette can be made 1 day ahead and refrigerated.)

Season both sides of the fillets with the Creole seasoning. Grill the fillets until just cooked through but still springy and soft to the touch, 4 to 5 minutes on each side.

In a large bowl, combine the remaining ingredients with the vinaigrette, reserving about 2 tablespoons of the vinaigrette. Toss well. Divide the salad among four plates, top with the fish, and drizzle with the reserved vinaigrette.

STREAM

Freshwater Bayous, Lakes, and Rivers

R EMEMBER WHEN YOU WERE A KID, and a walk through a park could turn into an African safari? Or how a deserted beach became a Robinson Crusoe adventure in your mind—just you against the elements? There's a grown-up chapter in that spirit going on here. You're on a boat, alone or with a friend, lost in your own world. You look for a secluded spot and pretend that *no one has ever fished there before.*

You ask yourself: What bait will I use? Will it be the perfect day? Is there too much wind or too little? What are the odds I'll catch a redfish? I'll make courtbouillon if I do. Or catfish? I'll fry 'em up.

The old saying is "They call it fishing, not catching." You just never know. Your experience improves the odds, but that's all. Success is always a question mark. You put a tiny baited hook into water that, more often than not, you can't even see into, and then you wait. You may reel in again and again, depending on the type of fish you are after, but mostly you wait. And wait.

Then *pop!* Something hits your line—no mistaking it. It's pulling and you're reeling. Now it's a scene from *The Old Man and the Sea.* Who will win? It may be only a measly catfish, but the surprise, the fight, and the anticipation are all a part of the thrill—an addictive thrill.

But sometimes you wait and wait and nothing happens. Not even a nibble. Sure, you'd rather catch something, but the other part of the fishing equation is all about just being on the boat, watching the sun dance across the water, listening to the quiet.

In the early stages of filming our show, *Off the Menu*, late chef Jamie Shannon, then sous-chef Danny Trace, and Lally Brennan took the Turner South film crew to catch redfish. They caught nothing. Nothing. We were losing time, money, and credibility.

They were on the way home empty-handed when they drove by a state park that Jamie knew had a big pier. It was late in the day and a bit overcast. Jamie just had this feeling that there were redfish around that pier. Not only did he have to convince the crew to stop to fish off the pier, but he also had to convince them to buy equipment. (They'd used the boat captain's equipment earlier that day.) You could see their eyes rolling. About fifteen minutes into it, *zing* went Jamie's line and he pulled in a bull redfish. Then another. And another.

It was a beautiful hunch and made for a great show and one happy producer. They cooked the fish right there on the pier—just-caught redfish courtbouillon. Now that's Louisiana.

Even after the ravages of Katrina, Louisiana is bountiful with crab, crawfish, redfish, trout, catfish, and other blessings from bayous, lakes, and rivers. You can prepare shellfish and fish in numerous ways, but none rival the fun of a backyard crawfish boil. Most common in the spring, when the crawfish are their tastiest and fattest, crawfish boils tend to be huge affairs, sometimes involving hundreds of pounds of spicy crawfish and equal amounts of beer to put out the fire.

You don't have to boil crawfish for a feast. Whole fish always transforms dinner into a feast, as it's so unexpected and special. Soft-shell crabs are equally celebratory, especially when you bite into your first one of the season. We adore soft-shells in Louisiana, and they can be purchased live at most seafood markets around the country from March on into the summer. Cooking with these beauties is both fun and easy; do it right and you'll never go wrong.

CRISPY SOFT-SHELL CRABS
WITH QUICK RAVIGOTE

Soft-shell crabs are one of Louisiana's fleeting delicacies, available only in the short time between the period when growing blue crabs shed their original shells and their new shells harden. Here in Louisiana, they usually are available from as early as March through September. Soft-shell crabs are also available up and down the East and Gulf coasts around this time. Don't bother with frozen ones, and plan to cook the crabs the day you buy them. To make a lunch out of this dish, serve the crab over salad greens and tomatoes. And you may never go back to plain tartar sauce after trying the bold flavor of our zippy ravigote.

Here, the frying crisps the outside coating and develops a seal so the crab can steam. For the sake of presentation, we fry crabs so that their claws stand up: Dip the claws into the oil first to set them, and then drop the entire crab into the oil.

• SERVES 4 •

QUICK RAVIGOTE

½ cup mayonnaise

¼ cup Creole mustard or other whole-grain mustard

1 large hard-boiled egg, chopped

1 tablespoon capers, chopped

1½ teaspoons chopped green onion (green part only)

¾ teaspoon prepared horseradish

Vegetable oil for frying

2 cups all-purpose flour

3 tablespoons Creole seasoning, store-bought or homemade (see box, page 9)

1½ cups fine dry bread crumbs

1 cup milk

2 large eggs

Four 3- to 4-ounce soft-shell crabs, cleaned (see box, page 53)

Prepare the quick ravigote: Whisk all the ingredients together in a medium bowl.

Fill a medium stockpot halfway with oil and heat it to 350°F.

Stir the flour and 2 tablespoons of the Creole seasoning together in a shallow bowl. Combine the bread crumbs and remaining 1 tablespoon Creole seasoning in another bowl. Whisk the milk and eggs in a medium bowl. Dredge each crab in the flour mixture, being sure to cover the underbelly and gill section. Then dip it in the egg mixture, and finally dredge it in the bread crumbs.

Fry 1 crab at a time: Holding a crab around its middle with tongs, dip the legs only (just about three-quarters of the way) into the hot oil and hold it there until the legs begin to crisp, 45 seconds. Turn the crab over and press it down to the bottom of the pot so that the back rests on the bottom and the belly is up. Hold the crab in this position by pressing the belly down with the tongs and cook until it is deep golden brown and cooked all the way through, 1½ minutes. While it is still hot, season the crab with salt and pepper. Repeat with the remaining crabs. Serve the crabs immediately, with the ravigote alongside.

FRYING FINESSE

The most important detail about frying is achieving and maintaining the proper temperature of the oil. If the oil is too hot, whatever you're frying will brown too quickly, and if it's too cool, you'll end up with soggy food. In between batches of frying, be sure to be patient and wait for the oil to come back up to the correct temperature, which is usually 350°F.

CLEANING LIVE SOFT-SHELL CRABS

Cleaning soft-shells isn't hard, but if you're squeamish, have the seafood market clean them for you. With kitchen scissors, cut off the mouth and eyes on each crab, and remove the brain. Lift the top shell on both sides and scrape or cut out the whitish gills with a small knife. Turn the crab over onto its back, pull down the triangular or T-shaped apron, and cut it away with scissors.

Soft-Shell Crab Bisque

Buy only live soft-shells, just like lobster—that way you're guaranteed they are fresh. And if you can't find soft-shells, certainly use hard-shell blue crabs. Crab paired with saffron creates a rich, delicious, and elegant soup.

• MAKES ABOUT 5 CUPS; SERVES 4 AS A FIRST COURSE •

5 tablespoons unsalted butter

¼ cup finely chopped onion

¼ cup finely chopped celery

¼ cup finely chopped shallots

14 ounces fresh soft-shell crabs, cleaned and chopped (see box, page 53)

1½ cups dry white wine

¼ teaspoon saffron threads

3 cups heavy cream

½ teaspoon kosher salt

½ teaspoon ground white pepper

2 large egg yolks

4 ounces jumbo lump crabmeat, picked over for shells and cartilage

In a stockpot, melt the butter over medium heat. Add the onion, celery, and shallots and cook until soft, 1½ minutes. Add the chopped crabs and cook until they are red and cooked through, 1½ to 2 minutes. Stir in the wine and saffron, bring to a boil, and cook until the wine is reduced by half, about 5 minutes. Add the cream, salt, and white pepper, and cook until the liquid is almost thick enough to coat the back of a spoon, about 10 minutes.

Puree the soup, in batches, in a blender until smooth. Strain it through a fine-mesh strainer into a medium saucepan, pressing against the solids with the back of a spoon to extract as much liquid as possible. Heat the soup over medium heat until hot, about 2 minutes.

Temper the egg yolks by placing them in a small bowl and slowly add about ½ cup of the soup, whisking to combine. Return the egg yolk mixture to the pot and stir well. Add the crabmeat to the soup and cook until just heated through, 1 to 2 minutes. Do not let this mixture come to a boil after adding the egg yolks or the eggs may curdle.

Marinated Crab Salad

This salad holds Ti's most powerful childhood taste memory. She spent her summers on the Mississippi Gulf Coast fishing, crabbing, swimming, water-skiing, and generally wreaking havoc with a gaggle of cousins, aunts, and uncles. The children had crab traps and would proudly carry their day's catch into the kitchen, where their Aunt Claire would drop them in a big ol' pot of seasoned boiling water. They all pitched in by cracking and picking crab for this salad. Ti's mouth waters just thinking about it. The crab is marinated in its shell and the meat is picked out of the shells at the table. It's messy eating, but darn fun.

• SERVES 6 AS A FIRST COURSE, OR 4 AS A MAIN COURSE •

2 heads garlic, minced

1 tablespoon garlic salt

1 tablespoon dried oregano

1 tablespoon dried parsley

1 tablespoon dried thyme

1 tablespoon dried basil

1½ cups vinegar (cane, cider, sherry, or red wine)

1 tablespoon extra virgin olive oil

2 medium onions, sliced thin

Kosher salt and freshly ground black pepper to taste

12 boiled crabs

1 pound new potatoes or other small potatoes, boiled, cooled, and sliced

4 Creole or vine-ripened tomatoes, sliced and seasoned with salt and pepper

Whisk the garlic, garlic salt, and dried herbs together in a large bowl. Whisk in the vinegar and oil. Add the onions and season with salt and pepper.

Clean the crabs by taking off their tops and removing the gills, which surround the cavity that contains the meat. Break the crabs in half and rinse away any debris. Discard the legs, remove and crack the claws, and add the cracked crab, still in its inner shell, to the marinade. Add the potatoes and toss. Marinate the salad, covered, in the refrigerator for 8 hours.

Serve the salad over the tomatoes.

Cajun Crawfish Alfredo

Simple and scrumptious, this pasta makes a great midweek dinner. It does call for a ton of cream, but an occasional creamy pasta alfredo can't be all bad.

• SERVES 4 •

8 ounces dried linguine

2 tablespoons vegetable oil

1 onion, diced

2 tablespoons minced garlic

3 teaspoons Creole seasoning, store-bought or homemade (see box, page 9)

3 cups heavy cream

1 pound cooked Louisiana crawfish tails

¾ cup freshly grated Parmesan cheese

2 bunches green onions (green part only), sliced thin

Bring a large pot of salted water to a boil. Add the linguine and cook until al dente, about 8 minutes. Drain.

Meanwhile, heat the oil in a large skillet over medium-high heat until it is hot and smoking. Add the onion and garlic, and sauté for 30 seconds. Add the Creole seasoning and sauté until the garlic starts to brown and the onion starts to caramelize, 1 minute. Stir in the heavy cream and cook until reduced by half, about 4 minutes.

Stir in the crawfish and cook for 2 minutes. Stir in the cheese and green onions, and cook, stirring, for 30 seconds. Add the pasta, tossing to coat it with the sauce, and cook until heated through, 30 seconds.

SALT-CRUSTED WHOLE REDFISH

The presentation of this dish belies its simplicity. Essentially we use nothing more than salt, which encases the fish, for seasoning. Chip off the salt crust to reveal a shockingly moist and tasty fish. The lemon-thyme oil is just a little extra flavor for drizzling over the fish at serving time.

• SERVES 4 •

LEMON-THYME OIL

¼ cup extra virgin olive oil

½ cup fresh lemon juice (2 large lemons), lemon halves reserved

4 sprigs fresh thyme

Pinch of freshly ground black pepper

Two 2-pound or one 6-pound redfish, gutted, rinsed, and gills (but not scales) removed

6 pounds kosher salt

Prepare the lemon-thyme oil: Heat the oil in a small skillet over medium-high heat until it is hot but not smoking, about 2 minutes. Add the lemon juice, lemon halves, thyme sprigs, and pepper. Cook, stirring occasionally, until fragrant, 1½ minutes. Remove the skillet from the heat and remove the lemon halves with tongs, squeezing them to extract as much liquid as possible. Discard the lemon halves and thyme sprigs, and set the oil aside until ready to use.

Preheat the oven to 450°F.

Pat the fish dry with a kitchen towel. Place a ¼-inch-thick layer of salt on a rimmed baking sheet that is large enough to keep the fish from hanging over the edges. Place the fish on top of the salt, and using your hands, mound the remaining salt so that it completely covers the fish. Roast the fish until an instant-read thermometer inserted into the thickest part of the fish registers 130°F, 28 minutes for 2 smaller fish, 1 hour for 1 bigger fish.

Brush the excess salt off the fish. You should have a hard white crust that encases the entire fish. Crack the top of the crust. With a fork, poke into the skin near the dorsal fin at the top of the fish, and run a tine of the fork under the skin up the back of the fish to the head, then in the opposite direction to the tail. Still using the fork, peel the skin back from the length of the fish, being careful not to let the fish flesh touch the salt. Using two large spoons, remove the top fillet and neatly place it on a serving platter. Remove the backbone by lifting it from the tail toward the head. Before removing the bottom fillet, push all the small fin bones off to the side. Remove the bottom fillet in the largest pieces possible, taking out any bones that you see.

Drizzle the fish pieces with the lemon-thyme oil, and garnish with a hunk of the salt crust.

CITRUS SALT–RUBBED REDFISH

This dish has evolved to become a best seller at Commander's Palace, and it's super-easy. All we do is make an intensely flavored salt by zesting citrus and combining the peels with salt and pepper in a spice grinder and voilà! Instant flavor. Double the salt recipe and keep it in an airtight container; it will add zest to pork, shrimp, and all sorts of fish.

At Commander's Palace, we serve this fish over roasted vegetables topped with a bed of raw fresh herbs. The herbs perfume the fish on the way to the table.

• SERVES 4 •

CITRUS SALT

Zest of 1 orange, in strips
Zest of 1 lemon, in strips
Zest of 1 lime, in strips
1 tablespoon kosher salt
2 teaspoons minced fresh thyme
¼ teaspoon crushed red pepper
   flakes

Four 6- to 8-ounce redfish fillets
2 tablespoons vegetable oil

Prepare the citrus salt: Combine all the ingredients in a spice grinder and pulse until well combined. (Alternatively, the salt can be made in a mortar and pestle.) (The citrus salt will keep in an airtight container at room temperature for up to 2 weeks.)

Preheat the oven to 450°F.

Place the fillets on a large baking sheet, rub with the oil, and season on both sides with the citrus salt. Roast for 7 to 8 minutes, until the fish is opaque and flaky to the touch.

No redfish? Substitute snapper, flounder, or speckled trout.

REDFISH GRIEG

This redfish dish was popular at Commander's Palace in the 1970s and '80s. We revisit it from time to time for its vivid flavor, and because it's so darn easy and quick to put together. Essentially it's just roasted fish topped with crabmeat and meunière sauce.

• SERVES 4 •

SAUCE

½ cup dry white wine

¼ cup Tabasco sauce

¼ cup Worcestershire sauce

1 medium lemon, peel and pith removed, chopped

1 shallot, chopped

2 sprigs fresh thyme

1 teaspoons minced garlic

Pinch of kosher salt, plus additional to taste

¼ teaspoon freshly ground black pepper, plus additional to taste

½ cup heavy cream

8 tablespoons (1 stick) cool unsalted butter, cut into pieces

Four 6- to 8-ounce redfish fillets

1 teaspoon plus a pinch of kosher salt

1 teaspoon ground white pepper

1 teaspoon minced garlic

½ teaspoon crushed red pepper flakes

6 tablespoons (¾ stick) unsalted butter, at room temperature

1 cup dry white wine

6 ounces jumbo lump or lump crabmeat, picked over for shells and cartilage

Pinch of freshly ground black pepper

Preheat the oven to 400°F.

Prepare the sauce: Heat a small saucepan over medium heat. Add the wine, Tabasco, Worcestershire, lemon, shallot, thyme, garlic, salt, and black pepper. Bring to a boil. Simmer until the sauce is reduced by three quarters, 5 to 6 minutes. Add the cream and bring back to a simmer. Simmer until the cream is reduced by half, 2 to 3 minutes. Reduce the heat to low and slowly whisk in the butter, one piece at a time, whisking constantly to form an emulsion. Adjust the seasoning, adding salt and pepper as needed. Strain the sauce through a fine-mesh strainer into a clean saucepan, pressing against the solids with the back of a spoon to extract as much liquid as possible. Keep it warm on the back of the stove.

Season the fish on both sides with the 1 teaspoon salt, white pepper, garlic, and red pepper flakes. Place in a baking dish. Spread 1 tablespoon butter over each fillet, and pour ¾ cup of the wine into the dish. Roast, uncovered, for 16 to 18 minutes, until cooked through.

In a small skillet, combine the remaining 2 tablespoons butter and the remaining ¼ cup wine, and bring to a boil over medium-high heat. Add the crabmeat, the pinch of salt, and the pepper. Toss to combine, being careful not to break up the lumps of crabmeat, until warmed through, about 1 minute. Spoon the crab mixture over the fish, and drizzle with the sauce.

GULF COAST COURTBOUILLON
WITH OYSTERS AND SHRIMP

When we were young and learning the history of Creole cooking, it was always interesting to find out that a dish that was so familiar had in fact a long, long history. Over our careers this dish has faded in and out of popularity, but you can find 1950s pictures of Miss Ella Brennan (Ti's mom) in her French Quarter days with grand copper pots full of Whole Baked Fish Courtbouillon. Courtbouillon is the French term for a flavorful poaching liquid for fish or shellfish, and literally means "short poaching liquid" (the "short" refers to the cooking time). Here in New Orleans we pronounce it "koobie-yawn."

We love to cook fish whole. Not only do the bones flavor the fish during cooking, but bringing the fish to the table always gets a round of applause.

• SERVES 6 TO 8 •

One 2½- to 3-pound whole redfish, gutted and scaled

2 tablespoons Creole seasoning, store-bought or homemade (see box, page 9)

1 tablespoon vegetable oil

¼ cup olive oil

4 cups chopped onions

2 cups chopped celery

1 cup thinly sliced garlic

4 green bell peppers, chopped

¼ cup seeded and minced jalapeño or serrano peppers

2½ pounds tomatoes, peeled, seeded, and diced

2 cups seafood stock, or a mixture of 1 cup water and 1 cup white wine

1 tablespoon Worcestershire sauce

1 tablespoon Tabasco sauce, or to taste

3 bay leaves

⅛ teaspoon saffron threads

1 pound large shrimp, peeled and deveined

1 pint shucked oysters in their liquor

2 tablespoons chopped fresh parsley

Preheat the oven to 450°F.

Rinse the fish under cold running water to remove as much blood and impurities as possible. With a knife, cut three deep slits on each side, down to the bone. Pat the fish dry with paper towels, and season on both sides with 1 tablespoon of the Creole seasoning. Brush the vegetable oil on a baking sheet, lay the fish flat on the sheet, and cook for 25 to 30 minutes, until a toothpick inserted near the spine slides out easily, without resistance.

Set a roasting pan that is large enough to hold the fish over two burners. Heat the olive oil in the pan over medium heat until it is hot but not smoking. Add the onions, celery, garlic, bell peppers, and jalapeños and cook, stirring, until the vegetables are lightly browned and tender, 10 minutes. Add the tomatoes, stock, Worcestershire, Tabasco, remaining 1 tablespoon Creole seasoning, bay leaves, and saffron, and stir well. Bring the mixture to a simmer and cook, stirring occasionally, until slightly reduced, 6 to 7 minutes. Lay the fish flat in the pan, arrange the shrimp and oysters around the fish, and bake in the oven for about 15 minutes, until the shrimp are pink and the oysters have curled. Sprinkle the parsley over the fish.

No redfish? Substitute snapper, sheepshead, or speckled trout.

Catfish Pecan

We love catfish, especially wild Catfish because it has great flavor and is so much fun to catch. As a boy, Tory would pretend that he had shark on his line instead of a catfish. Pecans are another Southern favorite, and their earthy flavor is threaded through this dish. We grind them up with flour and Creole seasoning to make a crisp, nutty crust, which is a welcome contrast to the tender catfish. The sauce is based on a classic New Orleans meunière sauce. New Orleans meunière has French roots but is a bit thicker than its French cousin and includes not just the traditional butter, garlic, thyme, and lemon but also Tabasco, Worcestershire, and bay leaf. We use olive oil instead of the usual sticks of butter in order to create a healthier, updated version of this classic.

• SERVES 4 •

1½ cups (about 7 ounces) pecan halves

1½ cups all-purpose flour

1 tablespoon plus 1 teaspoon Creole seasoning, store-bought or homemade (see box, page 9)

2 large eggs

½ cup milk

Four 6- to 8-ounce catfish fillets

½ cup vegetable oil

OLIVE OIL MEUNIÈRE SAUCE

5 tablespoons extra virgin olive oil

¼ cup minced mixed green, red, and yellow bell peppers

2 tablespoons minced shallot

¾ cup pecan halves

4 sprigs fresh thyme

2 medium lemons, halved

½ teaspoon Tabasco or other mild hot sauce

½ teaspoon Worcestershire sauce

1 teaspoon Creole seasoning, store-bought or homemade (see box, page 9)

Combine the pecans, flour, and 1 tablespoon Creole seasoning in the bowl of a food processor and pulse until smooth. Place the mixture in a large shallow dish. Beat the eggs and milk together in a large bowl.

Season both sides of the catfish with the remaining 1 teaspoon Creole seasoning. One at a time, dip the fish into the egg mixture, shake to remove any excess, and then dredge in the pecan-flour mixture, pressing to coat well.

Heat ¼ cup of the vegetable oil in a large skillet. Add 2 catfish fillets and cook until golden brown, about 3 minutes on each side. Transfer the fish to paper towels to drain. Repeat with the remaining fillets.

Prepare the olive oil meunière sauce: Drain the oil from the skillet and wipe it clean with paper towels. Return the skillet to medium-high heat. Add the olive oil, bell peppers, and shallot and cook, stirring, for 1½ minutes. Add the pecans and thyme and cook, stirring, until fragrant and lightly toasted, 2 to 3 minutes. Squeeze the lemon juice into the skillet and add the squeezed lemon halves, Tabasco, Worcestershire, and Creole seasoning. Cook, stirring, for 4 minutes. Remove the thyme sprigs and lemon halves. Serve the catfish drizzled with the meunière sauce.

PANFRIED RAINBOW TROUT
WITH LEMON AND THYME

This trout is utterly simple, yet über-tasty. With so few ingredients, the success of the dish relies on the technique and the quality of the ingredients. Tory first cooked this dish 10 hours north of the Canadian border in central British Columbia, on a 72-mile chain of lakes called the Mighty Bowron. It was there that he saw and helped catch the largest rainbow trout of his life, a 10-pound, 2-ounce monster that we nicknamed "Louie the Lunker." That trout fed fifteen people, and hangs today in the family log cabin in western Montana, near Yellowstone National Park.

• SERVES 4 •

2 cups all-purpose flour

¼ cup Creole seasoning, store-bought or homemade (see box, page 9)

Four 10- to 12- ounce rainbow trout, cleaned, scaled, and heads removed

12 tablespoons (1½ sticks) unsalted butter

4 sprigs fresh thyme

2 lemons, cut in half

Kosher salt and freshly ground black pepper

In a large bowl, combine the flour and Creole seasoning. Dredge the trout in the seasoned flour until dry on each side.

Heat a large skillet or 2 large skillets over medium heat. Add half of the butter and swirl until it is melted and bubbling. Add the trout and fry until they are cooked through and a toothpick passes easily through the thickest section, 3 to 4 minutes on each side. Transfer the trout to a platter.

Add the remaining 6 tablespoons butter to the skillet and swirl until it is mahogany brown and very nutty and fragrant. Remove the skillet from the heat and add the thyme; swirl for 5 seconds. Deglaze the skillet by squeezing the lemon juice into the skillet. Add the lemon halves to the sauce. Season the sauce with a pinch of salt and pepper. Serve the sauce, with the thyme sprigs and lemon halves, over the fish.

New Orleans Frog Legs Bordelaise

Cajuns have harvested frogs for years, and Creoles have prepared them in this classically French way as well. Tory likes to describe the taste of frog as "fishy chicken, but in a good way." We serve frog legs at Commander's Palace often, and they fly out the door. Don't be put off by the amount of butter called for here—this is an occasional treat, not an everyday dish.

• SERVES 4 AS A FIRST COURSE •

16 frog legs, cleaned

2 teaspoons Creole seasoning, store-bought or homemade (see box, page 9)

1 cup all-purpose flour

14 tablespoons (1¾ sticks) unsalted butter

2 tablespoons minced garlic

Juice of 2 lemons

¼ cup chopped fresh parsley

¼ cup thinly sliced green onions (green part only)

2 teaspoons Tabasco sauce

Place the frog legs in a bowl and season with the Creole seasoning. Sprinkle with the flour and toss with your hands until the frog legs are very dry and coated evenly.

Heat a large skillet over medium-high heat for 3 minutes, until hot but not smoking. Add 6 tablespoons of the butter and cook until completely melted. Remove the frog legs from the flour, shake to remove any excess, and fry, in batches, until golden brown, about 2 minutes on each side. As they are cooked, transfer the frog legs to a platter and keep warm.

Pour off any liquid in the skillet and wipe it clean with a paper towel. Add the remaining 8 tablespoons butter and the garlic and cook, stirring constantly, until the garlic and butter are golden brown and foamy, 3½ to 4 minutes. Stir in the lemon juice, parsley, green onions, and Tabasco, and cook for 30 seconds. Add the frog legs back to the pan, toss to coat, and heat through.

Swamp Wings (Buffalo-Style Frog Legs)

Tory was introduced to frog with this recipe, and he has loved frog ever since. If you like buffalo chicken wings, then you'll love these. You can turn up the heat by serving pepper jelly alongside for dipping.

• SERVES 4 AS A FIRST COURSE •

½ cup buttermilk

⅓ cup plus 2 tablespoons Crystal hot sauce

2 tablespoons Worcestershire sauce

16 frog legs, cleaned

2 shallots, finely chopped

6 garlic cloves, chopped

¼ cup heavy cream

6 tablespoons (¾ stick) unsalted butter

Vegetable oil for frying

2½ cups all-purpose flour

3 tablespoons Creole seasoning, store-bought or homemade (see box, page 9)

In a large bowl, whisk together the buttermilk, 2 tablespoons Crystal, and the Worcestershire. Add the frog legs and marinate in the refrigerator while you make the sauce.

In a small saucepan, combine the remaining ⅓ cup Crystal with the shallots and garlic, and cook over medium heat until reduced by half, 10 minutes. Swirl in

FROGGING

Most of us won't have to clean frog legs ourselves because we can find them at the market already cleaned, and if you're going frogging in the swamp, then the person who's taking you probably already knows how to clean them. But generally, "cleaned" frog legs are just the legs without any of the body. Tory has been frogging in the Florida Everglades and recommends that if you ever get the chance to do the same, wear a life jacket, because you're cruising on an airboat through the pitch black swamp in the middle of the night. Also be sure to hold the frogs right side up to prevent them from peeing on you—but if they do, it's all really just a part of the experience!

the cream and continue to cook until the sauce becomes thick, 4 to 5 minutes. Remove the saucepan from the heat and cool for 3 to 4 minutes. Finish the sauce by whisking in the butter until melted. Strain the sauce into a bowl, and keep warm.

Heat 3 inches of oil in a large pot to 350°F.

In a large bowl, stir together the flour and Creole seasoning. Remove the frog legs from the marinade, shaking off the excess, and dredge them in the seasoned flour until they are very, very dry, as if they were chicken wings. Fry the frog legs, in two batches, until they are crisp, golden brown, and cooked through, 3½ minutes. Transfer them to the bowl with the warm sauce, and toss to coat evenly.

NATCHITOCHES ALLIGATOR PIES

Natchitoches Meat Pies are famous—famous—around here. So this is dangerous territory. It's one of those dishes people don't dare emulate. But we're brave. After all, we (well, not Ti) go alligator hunting. That, of course, is a story all its own. Some of you may have even seen some of our alligator exploits on our Off the Menu *show on Turner South, when our chefs pull alligators into their boat. If it's scary to watch, imagine what it's like to participate in!*

If you have the time, a little sauce for dipping is tasty and super-quick here: In a small bowl, combine 1 cup honey with ½ cup Creole mustard and ¼ cup Jack Daniels. If you have any sauce left over, it is delicious with rabbit, grilled andouille sausage, and hot dogs.

• MAKES 8 PIES •

PIE DOUGH

2 cups all-purpose flour

½ teaspoon salt

1½ cups (3 sticks) cold unsalted butter, cut into small pieces

½ cup ice water

4 tablespoons (½ stick) unsalted butter

1½ tablespoons minced garlic

1 pound ground alligator meat

2 tablespoons hot or sweet paprika

1 tablespoon Creole seasoning, store-bought or homemade (see box, page 9), plus additional to taste

1 large onion, diced

2 celery stalks, diced

½ cup diced green bell pepper

¼ cup diced red bell pepper

¼ cup Jack Daniels bourbon or other bourbon

1 tablespoon chopped fresh thyme

2 tablespoons all-purpose flour

1 large egg, lightly beaten

Vegetable oil for frying

Prepare the pie dough: Combine the flour and salt in a medium bowl. With your fingers, incorporate the butter until the mixture resembles coarse crumbs. Add the ice water and work until the dough just comes together, being careful not to overwork it. Turn the dough out onto a lightly floured work surface and gently knead until it is smooth. Cut the dough in half, and form each half into a disk shape. Wrap them tightly in plastic wrap, and chill for at least 1 hour. (The dough can be prepared up to 5 days ahead.)

On a lightly floured surface, roll out each portion of dough to ⅛-inch thickness. Cut out eight 6-inch rounds. Place the dough rounds on a baking sheet lined with wax paper or plastic wrap, and chill until ready to assemble.

Melt the butter in a large skillet or saucepan over high heat. Add the garlic and cook until fragrant, 20 to 30 seconds. Stir in the alligator, the paprika, and the 1 tablespoon Creole seasoning and cook, stirring, until the meat is well browned and gives off its liquid, about 6 minutes. Drain in a colander set over a bowl and reserve 1 tablespoon of the drained liquid.

Return the skillet to high heat and add the reserved cooking liquid. Add the onion, celery, and bell peppers and cook, stirring, until caramelized, about 5 minutes. Stir in the Jack Daniels and thyme. Cook until the liquid has almost all evaporated, about 1 minute. Stir in the cooked alligator meat.

Remove the skillet from the heat and stir in the flour. Spread the filling on a baking sheet and let it cool. (To speed the cooling process, place the sheet in the freezer for 30 minutes.) Remove the dough from the refrigerator.

Lay the dough rounds on a lightly floured work surface and spoon ½ cup of the alligator filling on one side of each round, leaving a ½-inch border all around. With your finger, wet the border with the beaten egg. Fold the other side of the dough rounds over the filling and press the edges together to seal, forming a half-moon pie. Using a fork, crimp the edges. Place the finished pies on a baking sheet and refrigerate until ready to cook. (The pies can be prepared up to 2 days ahead.)

Fill a medium saucepan halfway with oil and heat it to 350°F.

Fry the pies, three at a time, turning them once, until golden brown, 3 to 4 minutes. Drain them on paper towels. Season with Creole seasoning.

No alligator? Substitute ground pork.

TURTLE SOUP

This dish is usually mentioned in the same sentence as "Commander's Palace." We are famous for it, but it can easily be made at home when you want a hearty soup to warm your bones.

• MAKES 5 QUARTS; SERVES 24 AS A FIRST COURSE, OR 12 AS A MAIN COURSE •

12 tablespoons (1½ sticks) unsalted butter

2½ pounds turtle meat, diced, or ground veal (beef or a combination of lean beef and veal stew meat may be substituted)

Kosher salt and freshly ground black pepper to taste

2 medium onions, diced

6 celery stalks, diced

1 large head garlic, minced

3 green bell peppers, diced

1 tablespoon ground dried thyme

1 tablespoon ground dried oregano

4 bay leaves

2 quarts veal stock or canned low-sodium chicken broth

1 cup all-purpose flour

1 bottle dry sherry (½ of 750 ml bottle)

1 tablespoon Tabasco sauce, or to taste

¼ cup Worcestershire sauce

Juice of 2 large lemons

3 cups peeled, seeded, and diced tomatoes

10 ounces fresh spinach, coarsely chopped

6 medium hard-boiled eggs, chopped

Melt 4 tablespoons of the butter in a large pot or Dutch oven over medium-high heat. Add the turtle meat, season with salt and pepper, and cook until the liquid has almost evaporated, 18 minutes. Stir in the onions, celery, garlic, bell peppers, thyme, oregano, and bay leaves and cook, stirring occasionally, until the vegetables are caramelized, 20 to 25 minutes. Add the stock and bring to a boil. Reduce the heat to low and simmer, uncovered, for 10 minutes, stirring occasionally and skimming away any fat that comes to the surface.

Meanwhile, prepare a roux by melting the remaining 8 tablespoons butter in a small saucepan over medium heat. Gradually add the flour, stirring constantly with a wooden spoon, and cook until nutty and pale, with the consistency of wet sand, 3 minutes.

Vigorously whisk the roux, a little at a time to prevent lumps, into the soup. Simmer the soup for 55 minutes, stirring occasionally to prevent burning. Add the sherry, Tabasco, and Worcestershire, and skim away any fat or foam that may rise to the surface while cooking. Add the lemon juice, tomatoes, spinach, and eggs, and bring back to a simmer. Adjust the seasoning with salt and pepper as needed. (The soup can be made up to 3 days ahead; cover and refrigerate. It can also be frozen for up to 1 month.)

No turtle? Substitute ground veal for "mock" turtle soup.

AIR

Everything Edible That Flies Overhead

Y OU'RE IN CAMOUFLAGE and you have your favorite gear. You're with
good friends—they're bleary-eyed and smell of strong coffee. It's 4 a.m.
You go outside. It's pitch black and eerily quiet. You set your decoys
while it's still dark and get into your blinds. You know that as morning breaks,
you'll have your best chance to call in some ducks.

You absorb the beauty and mystery of the land and water around you and quietly
savor it. The sky turns from night to day, and you watch it all come to life—stirring,
singing, flying.

Now you're huddled in your duck blind with your gun and dog at the ready.
The anticipation is at full throttle. (Hunters get what our friend Chef Danny
Trace calls "the terminator look.") You're still. Your eyes go from left to right,
constantly surveying, looking for any sign of motion. As sunlight peeks through
the dark, someone begins the duck calling. The dog tenses and watches your every move, waiting for the command. Your senses are keen. You smell salty, muddy
water and wet dog, gunmetal and oil, grass and wood.

You wonder: "What kinds of ducks will I get? A trophy mallard drake or the
mallard hen? Will I limit out? Will the dog find them?" You know that the jokes

will never end if you miss: "So, Tory, did your gun jam? That's all right, my dog couldn't carry any more."

Yes, hunters enjoy the challenge of shooting, but hunting is about so much more. When you ask a hunter why he likes to hunt, you will hear about the wonder of the outdoors, the respect for wildlife, and the camaraderie with family and friends. It's a complete day—a shared experience. And cooking your harvest is the 19th hole of hunting in Louisiana, always the best hole. Many people think duck, quail, goose, and other birds are restaurant food and therefore daunting, but these birds are actually easier to prepare than you think and will add vast variety to your cooking repertoire. These birds are pretty lean, especially if they are wild, and certain preparations work better than others. We keep lean meat moist by wrapping birds in batter, by braising birds in liquid until their meat is so tender it falls off the bone, by brining, and by marinating and then grilling quickly.

If you're a hunter and you're butchering the birds yourself, whatever you do, save the bones for stock. We believe that nothing should be wasted. If you're going to hunt and kill something, then use it all.

Chestnut-Crusted Dove Beignets with Sangria-Soaked Cherries

This is like dove tempura: The outside is crisp, with a hint of nuts from the chestnut flour, while the inside is still medium-rare and super-juicy. It makes a great hors d'oeuvre for your hunting buddies; they never dreamed that today's catch could be presented so elegantly.

• MAKES 30 BEIGNETS; SERVES 10 AS AN HORS D'OEUVRE •

Sangria-Soaked Cherries

1½ cups red wine

½ cup brandy

½ cup dried cherries

¼ cup sugar

Juice of 1 orange

Juice of 1 lemon

Vegetable oil for frying

Dove Beignets

¾ cup chestnut flour
(see box below)

¼ teaspoon sugar

¼ teaspoon kosher salt

¼ teaspoon baking powder

¾ cup club soda

1 egg, beaten

1 pound boneless, skinless dove breasts

1 tablespoon Creole seasoning, store-bought or homemade (see box, page 9), plus additional to taste

Prepare the sangria-soaked cherries: Combine all the ingredients in a small saucepan and cook over medium heat until the cherries are plump and the liquid is almost all evaporated, 25 minutes. (The cherries can be prepared 3 days ahead, covered, and refrigerated.) Keep warm.

Heat 3 inches of vegetable oil in a large pot to 350°F.

NUT FLOURS

Chestnut flour is a combination of regular wheat flour and ground chestnuts. We use it mostly in our pastry shop, but sometimes we borrow some for this dove dish. If you can't find chestnut flour at your supermarket, make your own by processing 2 parts all-purpose flour with 1 part roasted chestnuts.

Prepare the dove beignets: In a bowl, combine the chestnut flour, sugar, salt, and baking powder. Pour in the club soda and egg, and stir until smooth, about 30 seconds. Let the batter sit for 5 minutes to activate the baking powder.

Season the dove breasts with the Creole seasoning and dip them in the beignet batter to coat evenly on all sides. Fry, in batches, until lightly golden brown, about 1 minute. As they are cooked, transfer the beignets to paper towels to drain. Season with additional Creole seasoning if desired. Serve with the sangria-soaked cherries.

No dove breasts? Use squab or even beef from your butcher.

TORY'S TASTE

My favorite way to eat dove breasts is medium-rare because at this stage the meat is at its peak of juiciness and flavor. Cook your beignets just until they are a light golden brown; anything darker and the dove will be overcooked.

BACON-SEARED DUCK BREASTS OVER CRAWFISH POPCORN RICE

Wild ducks are so lean that we call for ample bacon fat for searing and for flavor. If you're using farmed breasts, which are much fattier, halve the amount of bacon fat.

• SERVES 4 •

CRAWFISH POPCORN RICE

4 tablespoons (½ stick) unsalted butter

1 onion, minced

1 tablespoon Creole seasoning,
   store-bought or homemade
   (see box, page 9)

1 teaspoon minced garlic

½ teaspoon kosher salt

1½ cups popcorn rice
   (see box, page 16), rinsed

2½ cups seafood stock or water

1 bay leaf

8 ounces cooked Louisiana crawfish
   tails

8 boneless, skin-on duck breasts
   (about 4 ounces each)

2 teaspoons kosher salt

1 teaspoon freshly ground black pepper

½ cup bacon fat

Prepare the crawfish popcorn rice: Heat a medium-size heavy saucepan over medium heat for 3 minutes. Add the butter, onion, Creole seasoning, garlic, and salt and cook, stirring occasionally, until the onion is translucent but not brown, 5 minutes. Stir in the rice and cook for 1 minute. Add the stock and bay leaf and bring to a simmer. Stir in the crawfish tails. Taste the liquid, and adjust the seasoning as necessary (you want the liquid to be well seasoned). Reduce the heat to low and cook, covered, until the rice is just tender, 10 minutes. Discard the bay leaf. Move the pan to the back of the stove and let the rice steam until tender, about 5 minutes. When the rice is cooked, fluff it with a fork so it does not become overcooked and sticky. Keep warm.

DUCK DO'S AND DUCK DON'TS

Ducks come in all shapes and sizes, and cooking times vary greatly depending on the type of duck you are cooking. The rule of thumb here is never to cook duck breasts past medium-rare. They are so lean that they will become dry and flavorless if cooked any longer. Adjust your cooking time as necessary for the size and type of your ducks.

Heat a large heavy cast-iron skillet over medium-high heat for 3 minutes, until it is hot but not smoking. Season the duck breasts on each side with the salt and pepper. Add the bacon fat to the skillet and heat for 30 seconds. Add the duck breasts, skin side down, and cook for 2 to 2½ minutes. Turn the duck breasts over and cook for 1½ to 2 minutes. Transfer the duck to a plate and let rest for about 5 minutes.

Slice the duck breasts, if desired, and serve with the rice alongside.

RICE TIPS

Cooking rice is a big deal in the Commander's kitchen. You have to do it right and season it right, and we find that the best-tasting rice comes from rinsing it first, then sautéing it in a lot of butter with onions and garlic, and cooking it in well-seasoned liquid. The liquid needs to have flavor up front because if you stir in the seasoning at the end, the rice will become sticky. The rice perfumes the whole kitchen and makes us all hungry. You can achieve the same results at home by doing it on the stove or by sautéing the ingredients before adding them to a rice cooker.

Roasted Goose and Andouille Gumbo

It's not exactly like shooting fish in a barrel, but let's just say that a slow-flying 8-pound goose coming in overhead is sort of like a 747 landing—not exactly a fighter jet. The southern flyway crossing Gueydan and Opelousas, Louisiana, is perfect goose-hunting territory.

We like Roasted Goose and Andouille Gumbo as a main course; it's as rich, flavorful, and satisfying a meal as any good sportsman could ask for. We find goose to be pretty lean and best prepared with moist cooking techniques like braising—or in a gumbo.

• MAKES 3½ QUARTS; SERVES 10 AS A MAIN COURSE •

One 8½-pound goose, rinsed well and patted dry

3 tablespoons kosher salt

1 tablespoon freshly ground black pepper

¾ cup vegetable oil

¾ cup all-purpose flour

3 cups chopped onions

3 cups chopped green bell peppers

3 cups chopped celery

3 tablespoons minced garlic

3 bay leaves

1 teaspoon dried thyme

1 pound andouille sausage, cut into ⅛-inch-thick half-rounds

3 quarts chicken stock or canned low-sodium chicken broth

3 cups cremini mushrooms, wiped clean and sliced

1 tablespoon Worcestershire sauce

1 tablespoon Tabasco sauce

1 tablespoon Creole seasoning, store-bought or homemade (see box, page 9)

Filé powder to taste

¼ cup thinly sliced green onions (green part only)

IS THERE A HUNTER IN THE HOUSE?

When butchering the day's catch, don't ever throw away the bones. Freeze them for later on, when you're home and have time to make a flavorful stock. This way nothing ever goes to waste.

Preheat the oven to 300°F.

Season all sides of the goose with the salt and pepper, and place it on a baking sheet. Roast for about 1 hour and 45 minutes, until it is cooked through and an instant-read thermometer inserted into the thickest part of the thigh registers 140°F.

Remove the goose from the oven and let it sit until cool enough to handle. Remove and discard the skin and fat. Remove the meat from the bones and coarsely chop it. Set the meat aside. (The meat can be covered and refrigerated for up to 2 days.) Reserve the bones for making stock.

Make a roux by heating the oil in a large stockpot or Dutch oven over medium-high heat until it is hot and shimmering. Gradually add the flour, stirring constantly with a wooden spoon, and cook until it is mahogany in color. Add the onions, bell peppers, celery, garlic, bay leaves, and thyme and sauté until the vegetables are soft, 10 minutes. Stir in the reserved goose meat and the andouille.

Gradually whisk in the stock, in a steady stream to prevent lumps, and bring to a simmer. Reduce the heat to medium and simmer for 1 hour, frequently skimming away any foam that rises to the surface.

Stir in the mushrooms, Worcestershire, Tabasco, and Creole seasoning. Remove from the heat and discard the bay leaves. (The gumbo can be made 3 days in advance; cover and refrigerate. Or freeze it for up to 1 month.)

Ladle the gumbo into large shallow bowls, and sprinkle about ¼ teaspoon filé powder over each bowl. Garnish with the green onions.

CREOLE STOCK

In a Creole kitchen, because our main emphasis is bold flavor, all of our stocks (except fish) are made from roasted bones, whether it be beef, chicken, veal, goose, lobster, or shrimp shells. By roasting the bones first, you get nice caramelization, which maximizes flavor even before you add water and aromatics.

APPLE AND BOURBON–
BRAISED PHEASANT

Pheasant has a kind of wild chicken flavor that most people enjoy. This dish epitomizes the fall hunting season with its natural combination of pheasant, apples, and whiskey, and is perfect for serving over Andouille Spoonbread (page 190).

• SERVES 4 •

8 pheasant legs with thighs (about
  1½ pounds total)

¾ teaspoon kosher salt

¼ teaspoon freshly ground black pepper

2 tablespoons vegetable oil

2 medium Gala apples, peeled, cored,
  and each cut into 8 pieces lengthwise

1 onion, cut into 6 pieces lengthwise

8 ounces button mushrooms, wiped
  clean, left whole

4 celery stalks, cut into 1½-inch pieces

2 carrots, halved lengthwise and cut
  into 1½-inch pieces

10 garlic cloves

¾ cup Jack Daniels bourbon

2 cups veal demi-glace (available at
  gourmet markets)

1 tablespoon chopped fresh thyme

2 tablespoons unsalted butter, cut into
  pieces

4 tablespoons chopped fresh parsley

Preheat the oven to 350°F.

Season the pheasant on both sides with ½ teaspoon of the salt and the pepper. Heat the oil in a large pot or large Dutch oven over high heat until it is hot and shimmering. Add half the pheasant legs, and cook until deep brown, 5½ to 6 minutes. Turn them over and cook for 4 minutes. Transfer to a plate. Repeat with the remaining pheasant legs, and transfer them to the plate. Add the apples, onion, mushrooms, celery, carrots, garlic, and remaining ¼ teaspoon salt to

SIZE OF WILD GAME VS. FARMED

Pheasant legs are generally pretty small, but again, the size depends on where you get them. Farm-raised pheasants will generally be larger than what you get in the wild.

the pot and cook, stirring occasionally, until the vegetables are caramelized, 10 minutes.

Add ½ cup of the Jack Daniels and cook, being very careful of flare-ups, until the liquid is almost evaporated, 1½ to 2 minutes. Stir in the demi-glace and bring to a simmer. Return the pheasant to the pot and bring the liquid to a simmer. Cover the pot, transfer it to the oven, and braise for about 1 hour and 30 minutes, until the meat is very tender and falling from the bone.

Remove the pot from the oven and set it on the stove over medium heat. Skim away any fat on the surface. Add the remaining ¼ cup Jack Daniels and the thyme, and cook for 5 minutes. Swirl in the butter until melted. Adjust the seasoning to taste, and garnish with the parsley.

No pheasant? Substitute grouse, a wild game bird abundant in the Rocky Mountains and the Midwest.

BRAISE IT, BABY

Braising is a simple cooking technique in which meat is caramelized with onions, garlic, and other aromatics and then simmered in liquid over low heat for a long time. This method is perfect for game because it breaks down the tough meat. The caramelization of the meat and vegetables, as well as the use of red wine and stock, boost flavor too. And with just a few hours, one pot, and hardly any work at all, you have a tender piece of meat with sauce as well.

Right: A rare quiet moment at Commander's front door . . .
Below: A world beyond . . .

*Above: Grilled Cobia with Shrimp
and Mango Salsa
Left: . . . even chefs can be cool . . .
Below: Sunset pulls us home*

*Left: Twenty-year
Commander's sous chef
Tom Robey . . . Do they
look alike? . . .
Below: . . . the magnifi-
cence of the underwater
world . . .*

Above: The freshest sushi you ever had . . . Costa Rican Tuna Poké

Right: . . . Louisiana shrimp boats at rest . . .

Above left: Just shucked . . . the way we like 'em
Above right: Dockside . . . chef Tory and chef de cuisine Chris Barbato basking in the day's success
Left: Parmesan-Crusted Oyster Salad—a new classic at lunch

Above: . . . the gang dives into a Louisiana crawfish boil. Below: A beautiful catch of Louisiana speckled trout. Right: . . . Lally lands one

Left: Hey, Tory—I think Lally got another one! Below: Crusty French bread, fresh Creole tomatoes, lightly fried speckled trout, and pickled okra . . . now that's a po' boy!

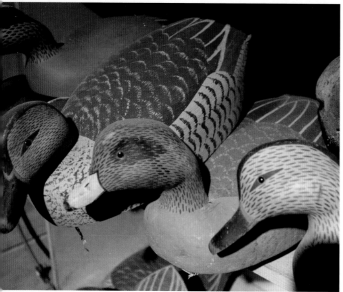

Top: Coffee-Lacquered Stuffed Quail
Above: Duck decoys
Right: Louisiana sportsman . . . in paradise

PECAN-ROASTED PHEASANT
WITH CHERRY GLAZE

Pecan butter keeps the lean and mild pheasant moist and adds a delectable taste and texture; the brandy and cherries create a fragrant glaze.

• SERVES 4 •

PECAN BUTTER

4 tablespoons (½ stick) unsalted butter,
  at room temperature
¼ cup finely chopped pecans
Pinch of kosher salt
Pinch of freshly ground black pepper

Four 5- to 6-ounce boneless, skin-on
  pheasant breasts
¼ teaspoon kosher salt
⅛ teaspoon freshly ground black pepper
1 tablespoon vegetable oil

CHERRY GLAZE

½ cup dried black cherries
2 teaspoons minced shallot
1 cup brandy
1 cup chicken stock or canned
  low-sodium chicken broth
2 tablespoons cold unsalted butter,
  cut into pieces
Kosher salt and freshly ground black
  pepper to taste

Prepare the pecan butter: Combine all the ingredients in a small bowl and mix until well combined. (The butter can be prepared up to 4 days ahead; cover and refrigerate.)

Preheat the oven to 350°F.

Pat the pheasant breasts very dry with paper towels and season on both sides with the salt and pepper. Heat the oil in a large ovenproof skillet over medium-high heat until it is hot and shimmering. Add the pheasant, skin side down, and cook until golden brown, 4 minutes. Turn the pheasant over and top with the pecan butter, using the back of a spoon to spread it over the skin. Transfer the skillet to the oven and roast for 15 minutes, until the pheasant is just cooked through. Transfer the skillet to the stove over high heat. Baste the pheasant with the butter from the skillet until the butter starts to brown, about 1 minute. Transfer the pheasant and browned pecan butter to a plate, cover with foil, and let rest for 5 minutes.

Prepare the cherry glaze: In the same skillet, combine the cherries and shallot and cook over medium heat, scraping to remove any bits, for 30 seconds. Remove the skillet from the heat and add the brandy. Return the skillet to the heat and carefully ignite the brandy; watch out for a possible flare-up. Cook the brandy until it is reduced by three quarters, about 2 minutes. Add the stock, bring to a simmer, and cook until it is reduced by half, about 2 minutes. Remove the skillet from the heat and swirl in the butter, a few pieces at a time, until melted. Adjust the seasoning with salt and pepper.

Drizzle the cherry glaze around the pheasant—not on top, as it would soften the crisp pecan topping.

SEARING SIZZLE

Getting a nice sear, or crust, on your food—whether it is game, beef, chicken, or fish—can be achieved only with extra-super-duper-dry food and a hot pan. If the meat is at all wet, you'll get a mediocre sear or, even worse, the food will steam.

GRILLED QUAIL WITH WILD RICE
AND FOIE GRAS BOUDIN

Not everybody is going to go hunting and then cook their quail with foie gras. But in New Orleans we wish we had a dollar for every time a regular customer of ours has told us about a grand meal they recently cooked with the thirty quails their group shot, or for every time a customer asks us to do a special, fancy meal with their wild game.

So you're not going to find this boudin on the side of the road, but the flavors here are Louisiana all the way. The boudin ingredients list may look daunting, but it's simple to assemble.

• SERVES 4 •

WILD RICE AND FOIE GRAS BOUDIN

12 ounces boneless pork butt, cut into ½-inch cubes

2¼ teaspoons kosher salt

1¼ teaspoons freshly ground black pepper

1 tablespoon vegetable oil

½ cup chopped onion

½ cup chopped celery

¼ cup chopped green bell pepper

¼ cup garlic cloves

½ teaspoon cayenne pepper

½ teaspoon Creole seasoning, store-bought or homemade (see box, page 9)

¼ teaspoon crushed red pepper flakes

4 bay leaves

3½ to 3¾ cups chicken stock or canned low-sodium chicken broth

1 cup wild rice

3 ounces foie gras, diced

¼ cup thinly sliced green onions (green part only)

2 tablespoons chopped fresh parsley

Four 5- to 6-ounce semi-boneless quails (all bones removed, except legs—see "Is there a hunter . . . ," page 88)

¼ cup olive oil

1 tablespoon minced shallot

¼ teaspoon chopped fresh parsley

¼ teaspoon chopped fresh thyme

¼ teaspoon chopped fresh rosemary

¼ teaspoon chopped fresh sage

½ teaspoon kosher salt

½ teaspoon freshly ground black pepper

We bone quails so that they're easier to eat. Use kitchen scissors to cut down both sides of the backbone and to snip the wings off by the breast. Push your thumb and forefinger between the breast meat and the bone and slowly pull the breast away from the carcass. Pull off the remaining rib cage and hip bones. Use a knife to remove any remaining bones in the breast, if necessary. At the restaurant, we leave the thigh and leg bones in the quail as a garnish. They don't contain a large amount of meat, anyway.

Prepare the wild rice and foie gras boudin: Season the pork butt with ¼ teaspoon of the salt and ¼ teaspoon of the pepper. Heat the oil in a large pot or Dutch oven over medium-high heat until it is hot and shimmering. Add the pork and sauté, stirring, until brown, 6 minutes. Stir in the onion, celery, bell pepper, garlic, cayenne, Creole seasoning, red pepper flakes, bay leaves, remaining 2 teaspoons salt, and remaining 1 teaspoon black pepper. Cook, stirring occasionally, until the vegetables are soft and caramelized around the edges, about 5 minutes. Add 2½ cups of the stock and bring to a boil. Reduce the heat and simmer, uncovered, until the pork is cooked and tender, about 45 minutes.

Set a large colander over a large bowl and strain the pork mixture into it, reserving the liquid. Remove the bay leaves and discard.

Pass the drained pork mixture once through a meat grinder fitted with a medium die, or pulse it in a food processor until the mixture is slightly chunky. Spread the mixture on a plate, cover with plastic wrap, and refrigerate until cold.

Place the reserved pork braising liquid in a small saucepan and add enough stock to measure 3½ cups. Bring to a boil. Stir in the wild rice and reduce the heat to low. Cook, covered, at a bare simmer until the rice begins to split open and becomes very sticky, 45 minutes to 1 hour. Drain the rice and stir in the cooked pork mixture and the foie gras, green onions, and parsley. Adjust the seasoning as necessary. This boudin can be made a day in advance or pushed to the back of the stove, covered, and kept warm until the quails are ready.

Preheat the oven to 350°F. Lightly grease a small rimmed baking sheet or a baking dish.

Place the quails on the prepared baking dish. Combine the oil, shallot, and herbs in a small bowl. Pour the mixture over the quails, cover, and marinate in the refrigerator for at least 1 hour and up to 24 hours.

Prepare a medium-hot fire in a grill.

Remove the quails from the marinade and season with the salt and pepper.

Place the quails on the grill, skin side down, and cook for 2½ minutes, being careful of flare-ups. Turn the quails over and cook on the second side for 2 minutes.

Divide the boudin mixture among four plates and rest the quails on top.

PORKY PLEASURE

Boudin is our favorite fast food, picked up at roadside shops in Cajun country and eaten before you can say "Big Mac and fries, please." The sausage, made of cooked pork, rice, onions, and seasoning, has a French ancestry, as do the Cajuns, and is a regional obsession with variations existing from parish to parish.

NICE WILD RICE

The consistency and cooking time of wild rice varies greatly depending on its freshness. You want the freshest rice possible, so purchase it from a reputable, high-volume market to help guarantee that the rice hasn't been hanging out on the lonely shelf for years.

ROASTED QUAIL WITH
BOURBON-BACON STUFFING

The men in the Brennan family hunt so much (as do most men, and lots of women, in southeast Louisiana) that it was inevitable that their restaurant life and their passion for hunting would collide. Years ago, we decided that we loved quail and wanted to have it on our menu permanently, but it was difficult to get a regular supply. No surprise then that it dawned on the Brennan men to ask a hunting friend, who was raising chickens and ducks, to raise quail for us. Quail has been on our menu regularly ever since.

While this quail roasts, it transfers flavorful juices to the moist bourbon stuffing underneath. If you'd like a little sauce to go with your quail, whisk together ½ cup Creole mustard, ¼ cup honey, ¼ cup warm water, and 1 tablespoon bourbon; drizzle it over the quail before serving.

• SERVES 4 •

BOURBON-BACON STUFFING

3 ounces lean boneless pork, such as tenderloin, coarsely chopped

2½ ounces boneless quail meat, coarsely chopped

2 slices bacon, coarsely chopped

½ tablespoon bourbon

½ tablespoon ruby port

½ teaspoon chopped fresh thyme

½ teaspoon chopped fresh sage

Pinch of kosher salt

Pinch of freshly ground black pepper

¼ cup chopped pecans

Four 5- to 6-ounce semi-boned quails (see "Is there a hunter . . . ," page 88)

½ teaspoon kosher salt

¼ teaspoon freshly ground black pepper

Prepare the bourbon-bacon stuffing: Combine all the ingredients except the pecans in a medium bowl, and toss well. (The stuffing can be made up to this point 1 day ahead; cover and refrigerate.) Pass the stuffing twice through the smallest die of a meat grinder, keeping the ingredients as cold as possible. (Alternatively, pulse the stuffing ingredients in a food processor until nearly smooth.) Transfer the stuffing to a clean bowl and fold in the pecans.

Preheat the oven to 350°F.

Divide the stuffing into four equal portions, form each into a ball, and transfer them to a work surface.

Season both sides of the quails with the salt and pepper. Drape each quail over a ball of stuffing, wrapping it around the stuffing to resemble a whole quail. Transfer the quails to a baking sheet and roast for 20 to 25 minutes, until an instant-read thermometer registers 140°F. Remove the quails from the oven and let rest in a warm area for 10 minutes.

COFFEE-LACQUERED STUFFED QUAIL

We don't imagine that there is a restaurant in the U.S. that has served more quail or served it in more ways than we have at Commander's Palace. The bold, rich flavor of quail is a perfect match for this tangy cane syrup and coffee glaze, while the custard-like bread pudding with chopped apples is irresistible as stuffing. Bacon-Smothered Green Beans (page 193) are a great choice for rounding out the meal.

The consistency and cooking time of the lacquer is determined by the quality of the veal stock. The more gelatinous the stock, the richer and thicker the lacquer will be. Veal stock can be purchased at your local gourmet market. Don't be tempted to save time by making the lacquer with hot coffee; it will be bitter.

• SERVES 4 •

COFFEE LACQUER

¼ cup freshly ground chicory coffee

¾ cup veal stock

⅓ cup Steen's pure cane syrup (see Resources, page 218) or blackstrap molasses

¼ cup sliced shallots

2 teaspoons Jack Daniels bourbon or other bourbon

STUFFING

2 tablespoons unsalted butter

2 cups peeled and chopped Granny Smith apples

1 cup finely chopped onions

½ cup finely chopped green bell pepper

½ cup finely chopped celery

1 tablespoon chopped fresh sage

1 bay leaf

Kosher salt and freshly ground black pepper

¾ cup heavy cream

1 large egg

4 cups cubed stale French bread (1-inch cubes)

Eight 5- to 6-ounce semi-boned quails (see "Is there a hunter . . . ," page 88)

1 teaspoon Creole seasoning, store-bought or homemade (see box, page 9)

Prepare the coffee lacquer: Combine 1 cup cold water and the ground coffee in a measuring cup, stir well, and let steep for 1 hour. Line a fine-mesh strainer with a coffee filter, and strain the cold-brewed coffee into a glass measuring cup. Set it aside.

We are very, very serious about our coffee in New Orleans. Long before the present Starbucks-driven coffee craze, we served strong coffee that was right on the money to our locals and shocking to visitors. At Commander's Palace, we serve French Market Coffee (see Resources, page 219) and chicory, which has a flavor we find unmatched.

In the kitchen we all drink gallons of coffee. No wonder that it would end up in the food one day in a happy "chocolate crashes into peanut butter" moment. Some taste combinations simply elevate one another to a higher level.

Combine the veal stock, cane syrup, and shallots in a medium saucepan and bring to a simmer. Reduce the heat and simmer until thick and reduced to about ¼ cup, about 20 minutes. Strain the mixture into a clean bowl, and whisk in the reserved coffee and the Jack Daniels. (The lacquer can be made up to 3 days ahead; cover and refrigerate.)

Preheat the oven to 350°F. Lightly grease a medium baking sheet and set it aside. Bring 2 cups of water to a simmer in a medium saucepan over medium-high heat. Set out a shallow heatproof bowl that will sit on the saucepan without touching the water.

Prepare the stuffing: Heat a large skillet over medium-high heat for 1 minute. Add the butter, and when it has melted, add the apples, onions, bell pepper, celery, sage, bay leaf, and a pinch each of salt and pepper. Sauté until the onions are translucent and all the vegetables are tender, about 5 minutes. Set the skillet aside.

In the reserved heatproof bowl, whisk together the cream, egg, and a pinch each of salt and pepper. Place the bowl over the simmering water, ensuring that the bottom of the bowl does not touch the water, and cook the custard, whisking constantly, until it is thickened enough to coat the back of a spoon, about 4 minutes. Remove the bowl from the heat and continue to whisk constantly for 2 minutes to help cool the mixture.

Place the bread cubes in a large bowl and pour the custard over them, combining well with a rubber spatula. Add the sautéed vegetables, stirring to combine. Let sit for 5 minutes.

Place the quails on a work surface and season both sides with the Creole seasoning. Divide the stuffing into eight equal portions and roll each one into a ball. Drape each quail over a ball of stuffing, wrapping it around the stuffing to resemble a whole quail. Place the quails on the prepared baking sheet and roast for 20 minutes. Remove the baking sheet from the oven, and using a pastry brush, paint the lacquer onto the quails. Return the sheet to the oven for 30 seconds to set the lacquer. Repeat the lacquering until a dark, glossy coat develops. Drizzle the remaining lacquer over and around the quails.

ORANGE-BRINED TURKEY BREAST
WITH SPICY CITRUS COMPOTE

Growing up, we never found that the holiday turkey or beef roasts tasted particularly good—they were very bland and had little seasoning. We compensated for this in following years by doubling the seasoning, which made the outside even drier and almost inedible. No wonder everyone gets stressed and freaked out when cooking for fifteen to twenty people.

If you want to add more flavor to your cooking and discover a newfound confidence in cooking large pieces of meat, you need to fully understand this technique. It's a simple process called brining.

Today we soak large cuts of meat in a combination of water, salt, sugar, and any accent of flavors to our liking. We also inject the center of the meat with the solution so the inside soaks up some of that great seasoning as well. As a basic rule, the larger the cut, the longer the brine; the longer the brine, the lower the salt. Not to get too technical, but through brining, a layer of proteins and amino acids will be exposed on the outside surface of the meat. This thin film is called a pellicle skin, and it acts as "flavor traction." This means your meat will pick up more flavor at a much faster pace than if you didn't brine it.

No matter whether you are smoking, roasting, sautéing, frying, or braising next, use this little trick to your advantage, and get results that you used to see only in books and magazines.

A SHOT OF FLAVOR

Injecting meats with a flavorful mixture adds 2 days of brining flavor in just 2 hours. At Commander's Palace we inject lean veal tenderloins with smoky bacon fat, duck breasts with sour cherry–Sazerac sauce, and pork roasts with coffee and local sugarcane. Be as creative as you like—your family and friends will be thrilled with the best-tasting food they've ever had from your kitchen.

Boneless breasts of one 12-pound
    turkey, or two 1¼-pound boneless
    breasts with skin on

4 cups fresh orange juice

1½ cups dark brown sugar, packed

2 tablespoons kosher salt

2 tablespoons very finely ground black
    pepper

Large kitchen injector (available at
    kitchen shops)

2 tablespoons vegetable oil

SPICY CITRUS COMPOTE

2 pounds oranges, peel and pith
    removed

¼ cup sugar

¼ cup Grand Marnier

1½ tablespoons seeded and minced
    jalapeño pepper

2 teaspoons finely grated lemon zest

2 teaspoons finely grated orange zest

Place the turkey breasts in a large nonreactive bowl or pan. In another bowl, whisk together the orange juice, brown sugar, 1 tablespoon of the salt, and 1 tablespoon of the pepper. Pour this over the turkey. Fill the injector with the brine and inject it all over, at least 10 times in each breast. Cover the bowl and refrigerate the turkey for at least 2 hours and up to 12 hours.

Preheat the oven to 400°F.

Place the turkey breasts on a work surface and pat them dry repeatedly with kitchen towels (paper towels will stick to the turkey). It's critical that the turkey is as dry as possible; otherwise the skin will stick to the pan and burn.

Season the turkey breasts on both sides with the remaining 1 tablespoon salt and 1 tablespoon pepper. Heat the vegetable oil in a large, heavy, ovenproof skillet or roasting pan over medium-high heat until it is hot but not smoking, about 3 minutes. Add the breasts, skin side down, and sear until deep brown, about 5 minutes. Turn the breasts over, then transfer the skillet to the oven and roast for about 20 minutes, until an instant-read thermometer inserted into the thickest part of the breast registers 135°F. Remove the skillet from the oven and transfer the turkey from the pan to a baking sheet and let rest covered for 15 minutes before carving.

Meanwhile, prepare the spicy citrus compote: Holding an orange over a bowl, to collect the juices, run a sharp knife alongside the white membranes to remove the segments. Reserve the segments in another bowl. Repeat with the remaining oranges. Combine the orange juice, sugar, Grand Marnier, jalapeño, and lemon and orange zests in a medium saucepan and bring to a boil. Reduce the heat and simmer until the mixture is reduced to about ½ cup and large bubbles are beginning to appear on top, 11 to 12 minutes. Stir in the orange segments and remove from the heat. (The compote can be made up to 1 day ahead; cover and refrigerate.)

Slice the turkey and serve with the compote.

ROASTED TURKEY WITH GIBLET GRAVY AND OYSTER DRESSING

Thanksgiving is a huge holiday for us at Commander's Palace, and about 80 percent of our guests order this turkey. The turkey has to be right—but for us it's all about the oyster dressing. Everyone has a special dish without which it wouldn't be the holidays. Well, this is ours. You'll have extra gravy here, so we suggest heating it up and drizzling it over homemade biscuits the morning after.

• SERVES 10 TO 12 •

One 12- to 14-pound turkey

1 cup (2 sticks) unsalted butter, at room temperature

2 tablespoons vegetable oil

3 tablespoons kosher salt

1 tablespoon freshly ground black pepper

Oyster Dressing (recipe follows)

1½ cups all-purpose flour

½ cup diced onion

½ cup diced celery

½ cup diced green bell pepper

2 teaspoons minced garlic

1 bay leaf

1 quart chicken stock or canned low-sodium chicken broth

2 tablespoons chopped fresh sage

Pinch of ground white pepper

Remove the giblets, liver, heart, and neck from the turkey, and rinse them well. Pat dry and set aside. Let the turkey come to room temperature for 1 hour. Preheat the oven to 450° F.

Pat the turkey dry all over with paper towels. Rub the butter under the skin of the turkey, working outward to the thighs as much as possible, being careful not to tear the skin.

Rub the oil all over the turkey. Season inside the turkey cavity and on both sides with 2 tablespoons of the salt and the pepper. Lay the bird, breast side down, on a rack in a large roasting pan. Add the turkey neck to the pan. Tie the legs together with butcher's twine. Roast, uncovered, for 30 minutes. Carefully turn the turkey over and roast, breast side up, for 1 hour, until the turkey is cooked through and an instant-read thermometer inserted into the thigh reaches 140°F.

While the turkey is roasting, prepare the Oyster Dressing.

When the turkey is done cooking, transfer it to a platter and tent it with foil to keep it warm.

Scrape all the bits from the bottom of the roasting pan with a wooden spoon. Pour the pan juices into a large saucepan. You need 1½ cups of liquid. (Save the remaining pan juices for soup or to drizzle across the sliced turkey to keep it moist when serving.) Whisk in the flour. Stir in the onion, celery, bell pepper, garlic, and bay leaf and cook, stirring, for 3 minutes. Next, chop the giblets, liver, and heart; and add them, along with the turkey neck, to the vegetables. Whisk in the stock, bring to a simmer, and cook, skimming the surface to remove all fat and impurities, for at least 20 minutes or up to 1 hour. (The flour taste from the roux is completely gone after 60 minutes of cooking.) Season the gravy with the remaining 1 tablespoon salt, the sage, and the white pepper.

Strain the gravy through a fine-mesh strainer into a gravy boat, and cover to keep it warm until ready to serve.

Reheat the turkey in a 350°F oven right before serving to ensure that it's piping hot all the way through.

IS THERE A HUNTER IN THE HOUSE?

Wild turkey doesn't have the plump breast meat of a farmed bird, so if you're feeding a bunch of family members at Thanksgiving, augment your whole wild bird with a farmed breast. When making gravy from the roasted wild bird, you might need to add a little butter for richness, since the wild bird is pretty lean.

OYSTER DRESSING

You say stuffing, we say dressing—it's a regional thing. The side dishes passed down from generation to generation are what Thanksgiving taste memories are all about. Oyster Dressing is one that for us is a marriage of flavors that elevate these humble ingredients perfectly.

4 tablespoons (½ stick) unsalted butter

3 celery stalks, diced

2 small onions, diced

1 green bell pepper, diced

5 garlic cloves, minced

1 jalapeño pepper, seeded and minced

2 tablespoons poultry seasoning

3 cups shucked oysters in their liquor

16 cups cubed crisp French bread (1-inch cubes)

1 cup chicken stock or canned low-sodium chicken broth

4 large eggs, beaten

Kosher salt and freshly ground black pepper to taste

2 cups chopped fresh parsley

½ tablespoon chopped fresh rosemary

2 green onions (green part only), sliced thin

Melt the butter in a large pot over medium heat. Add the celery, onions, bell pepper, garlic, jalapeño, and poultry seasoning. Cook until the vegetables turn brown and are tender, 15 minutes. Add the oysters and their liquor, and cook until the oyster edges curl, 4 to 5 minutes. Turn off the heat and stir in half of the bread cubes, letting them soak up any liquid. Add the stock and stir. Add the remaining bread cubes and stir. Add the eggs quickly, stirring constantly to be sure the eggs don't cook when they hit the hot vegetable mixture. Season with salt and pepper. Stir in the parsley, rosemary, and green onions. The stuffing should be moist but pliable, damp but not wet. If it's too wet, add more bread; if it's too dry, add more liquid.

Grease a 9×13-inch baking pan. Transfer the dressing to the pan and cover it with aluminum foil. If there's room in the same oven where the turkey is roasting, bake the stuffing for 20 minutes; then remove the foil and bake for another 5 minutes, until a thermometer inserted in the center registers 140°F. Alternatively, bake the stuffing, covered, in a preheated 350°F oven for 30 minutes; then remove the foil and bake for another 5 minutes, until a thermometer inserted in the center registers 140°F.

LAND

Big, Bold Flavors for Wild Beasts

THE LOUISIANA LICENSE PLATE reads "Sportsman's Paradise." They are not talking about golf or football, even though we do love our Saints. They are talking about fishing and hunting. When you fly into New Orleans you see miles of soupy land, tall grass, and cypress stumps. Farther inland, the acres of forests and brush spotted with ponds and waterways are that sportsman's paradise. Wildlife, from deer to rabbit to wild boar, thrives within an hour of the city.

Regular hunting is easily accessible throughout the Southeast, but Louisiana chefs will go a long way to catch the biggest tuna or bag a bear. Tory traveled to Costa Rica because of the lure of deep-sea fishing. North Carolina beckoned for a bear hunt, and Argentina is Alex Brennan-Martin's country of choice for duck hunting.

Hunting is a lifestyle for many people in much the same way golf is. Golfers plan trips with friends, get up early in the morning to hit a few, dream about the next course they'll play, and spend lots of time talking about the sport and the beautiful outdoors. They plan their life around it as much as they can.

Substitute the word *hunters* for *golfers* and you have much the same scenario. Both are enthusiasts who love their sport and the camaraderie involved, and who share a reverence for the outdoors.

Maybe that comparison is a way for non-hunters to better understand hunters. The actual harvesting of the animal is not why people hunt. They are true outdoorsmen, and with that comes an understanding that the package in the grocery store comes from somewhere. Hunters don't struggle with the balance between man and nature.

Children of outdoorsmen are raised in an environment where hunting and fishing and learning about wildlife, the environment, and safety are just a natural part of life. They look forward to the day when they can participate in a real hunt, much as other children eagerly anticipate getting their drivers' licenses.

Shooting a buck with a full rack of antlers is the thrill of a lifetime for many hunters. I know of one family in which a young girl shot two grand bucks in one season, meaning her father couldn't shoot any more. I know her father was thrilled for her, but I'm sure that he was also a little envious—kind of like the child golfer getting a hole in one before Dad.

People always want to know if venison tastes "gamey." Our answer is, "Gloriously, yes!" All game is not created equal—a deer is not an elk is not a rabbit. Each has its place in the world of hunting and at the table, and we revel in those differences.

The cooking methods and recipes we've learned along the way are just as prized as the hunting itself. We believe that big-flavored game, such as venison and elk, needs big-flavored ingredients. We often pair game with serious spices like Creole seasoning and intense flavors such as red wine. Because wild game is so much leaner than farm-raised, it needs to be cooked or grilled just to medium-rare to stay juicy and tender. Another preparation that works wonders for lean game is a long, slow turn in the oven—rich gravies are created that way, and the meat becomes super-tender. Allowing the meat to rest before slicing is another good tip for retaining moisture. The good news, of course, is that you don't have to be a hunter to have access to game. It is now widely available at supermarkets because savvy consumers prize it for being low fat and tasty.

LAND

BLACKENED VENISON STEAKS WITH BACON MASHED TURNIPS AND RED WINE–BLACK PEPPER SYRUP

This recipe is a great example of our food philosophy at Commander's Palace: a balance of flavors and seasoning based around the main ingredient. Take it a step further and try to coordinate the rest of the meal around the main dish. As an example, we wouldn't serve delicate crabmeat as an appetizer here; we'd opt for Roasted Goose Andouille and Gumbo instead. Choose your wines in the same way, and remember to lift your glass to the hunter who took down the game.

• SERVES 4 •

BACON MASHED TURNIPS

⅔ cup chopped bacon

1 cup chopped onions

1 pound small turnips, chopped

3 cups milk

2 tablespoons unsalted butter, at room temperature

Kosher salt and freshly ground black pepper to taste

RED WINE–BLACK PEPPER SYRUP

½ cup dry red wine

½ cup Steen's pure cane syrup (see Resources, page 218)

¼ teaspoon freshly ground black pepper

Four 8-ounce venison steaks, about ½ inch thick

4 teaspoons Creole seasoning, store-bought or homemade (see box, page 9)

4 teaspoons vegetable oil

Prepare the bacon mashed turnips: Heat a medium saucepan over medium heat. Add the bacon and cook, stirring, until the fat is rendered and the bacon is just beginning to color, 4 minutes. Add the onions and cook, stirring occasionally, until soft, 4 minutes. Add the turnips and milk, bring to a simmer, and cook until the turnips are tender, about 45 minutes.

Drain the turnips in a colander set over a bowl; the milk can be saved if you like. Return the turnips to the pan and add the butter, salt, and pepper. Stir vigorously with a heavy wooden spoon until roughly mashed. Keep warm until ready to serve.

Prepare the red wine–black pepper syrup: Combine the wine and cane syrup in a small saucepan and bring to a simmer over medium heat. Reduce the heat to medium-low and simmer gently until reduced by two thirds, about 18 minutes. Remove from the heat, stir in the pepper, and let cool to room temperature before serving.

Pat the venison steaks dry with kitchen towels (paper towels will stick to the meat). Sprinkle the Creole seasoning on both sides of the steaks. Heat a large cast-iron skillet over medium-high heat until it is very hot and just smoking, 4 to 5 minutes. Add the oil, swirling to coat the bottom of the skillet. Add the steaks and sear until dark brown, 3 to 4 minutes. Turn the steaks over, reduce the heat to medium, and sear for 3 to 4 minutes for medium-rare. Transfer the steaks to a platter and let rest for 5 to 10 minutes. Serve the steaks drizzled with the sauce, with the turnips alongside.

IS THERE A HUNTER IN THE HOUSE?

Nothing gets our goat more than letting game go to waste by improper handling. Don't just wrap the meat up and store it in a cooler of ice. Before we go hunting, we *always* have a plan in place regarding how we'll transport and store the meat. The goal is to hang and chill the venison as quickly as possible. We use a facility near where we hunt that is large enough for aging the venison in cold storage for up to 6 weeks to tenderize it. If this is not possible or practical, then cool the venison to below 40°F as quickly as possible, and butcher it as you would a cow: Save all the steaks from the backstrap (the loin), save the hind legs for thin cutlets and roasts, and save the front legs for sausage. Many game hunters have butchers they know and trust who do this for them.

MUSHROOM-CRUSTED VENISON WITH FOIE GRAS–SMOTHERED BLACK-EYED PEAS

Go ahead—show off a little. You deserve it, and your guests will be impressed because not only can you hunt, you can cook! This is a point of pride for all the hunters we know. If this dish sounds too fancy for you, you can certainly omit the foie gras, but we find that taking a luxury item like foie gras and adding it to something as humble as black-eyed peas transforms the whole dish into something new and unexpected. Foie gras butter is sold at gourmet markets, and it's less expensive than straight foie gras, with all the flavor and richness.

• SERVES 4 •

FOIE GRAS–SMOTHERED
BLACK-EYED PEAS

1 cup dried black-eyed peas

1 tablespoon vegetable oil

3 ounces tasso, chopped (½ cup)
(see box, page 10)

½ cup chopped onion

1 teaspoon minced garlic

½ cup chopped green bell pepper

¼ cup chopped celery

1 teaspoon plus 1 tablespoon chopped
fresh thyme

About 3 cups chicken stock or canned
low-sodium chicken broth

8 ounces foie gras butter (available at
gourmet markets)

1¼ teaspoons kosher salt

2 ounces dried wild mushrooms

1 teaspoon kosher salt

1 teaspoon freshly ground black pepper

2 pounds boneless white-tailed deer
backstrap, cut into 4 steaks

1 tablespoon vegetable oil

2 tablespoons unsalted butter

Prepare the foie gras–smothered black-eyed peas: Place the peas in a medium bowl and cover with water. Let stand for 2 hours. Drain in a colander and set aside. Heat the oil in a medium saucepan over medium-high heat. Add the tasso and cook, stirring occasionally, for 2 minutes. Add the onion and garlic and cook, stirring, for 2 minutes. Add the bell pepper and celery and cook, stirring, for 2 minutes. Add the black-eyed peas, 1 teaspoon thyme, and enough stock to cover the peas by ¼ inch; bring to a boil. Reduce the heat and simmer until the peas are tender and slightly creamy, 40 to 45 minutes.

Remove the pan from the heat and add the foie gras butter, several spoonfuls at a time, stirring to incorporate. Stir in the remaining 1 tablespoon thyme and the salt. Keep warm on the back of the stove.

Place the mushrooms, salt, and pepper in a spice grinder or a mini processor and pulse until ground to a powder. Transfer the powder to a large plate and add the venison steaks, turning to coat them evenly on both sides.

Heat a large cast-iron skillet over medium-high heat until it is hot but not smoking. Add the oil and swirl to coat the bottom of the skillet. Add the butter, and when it has melted and is lightly browned and foamy, add the steaks. Sear until deep brown, 2½ minutes on each side for medium-rare. Transfer the steaks to a cutting board and let rest for 5 to 10 minutes. Serve the steaks with the black-eyed peas alongside.

JUNIPER BERRY–GRILLED ELK

Tory is from Ferndale, Washington—"five minutes from the water and five minutes from Canada," as he likes to say. He grew up with the area's long tradition of hunting and fishing and talks with awe about the beauty of an elk hunt. Majestic *is his word. "You're up well before dawn. It's cold, there's snow on the ground, and a year's worth of nervous anticipation is welling up in your stomach. After parking the truck or the four-wheelers, we walk quickly to our spots through the frozen darkness. As we get ourselves situated, I'm always amazed at how quiet it is. Then, after thirty or forty minutes the darkness turns to light and again I'm amazed at how loud the forest can sound as it wakes. Majestic, pristine surroundings, the smell of damp earth, enough light now to see the whole meadow and surrounding thickets. The scene is set for a Rocky Mountain elk hunt."*

Elk meat is a deep reddish purple and so very lean that you must cook it only to medium-rare to ensure the proper easy-to-chew texture and moist flavor. Juniper berries and herbes de Provence lend herbal notes to the elk, while the fresh blackberries brighten the palate between bites of meat.

• SERVES 4 •

JUNIPER SPICE RUB

1 tablespoon plus 1 teaspoon juniper
   berries (available at gourmet
   markets)

2 teaspoons whole black peppercorns

1 teaspoon herbes de Provence

2 teaspoons kosher salt

4 ounces fresh blackberries

2 tablespoons sugar

2 tablespoons vegetable oil

1¼ pounds elk sirloin, cut into
   4 steaks

Prepare the juniper spice rub: Combine the juniper berries, peppercorns, and herbes de Provence in a spice grinder and process to a powder. Add the salt and pulse one more time. Set aside. (The juniper spice blend will keep in an airtight container at room temperature for up to 3 weeks.)

Prepare a hot fire in a grill.

Combine the blackberries and sugar in a small bowl, and let sit for 10 minutes.

Drizzle the oil over the elk, and season both sides with the spice rub. Grill until medium-rare, 3 to 4 minutes on each side. Transfer the elk to a cutting board and let rest for 3 minutes. Serve the elk topped with the blackberries.

No elk in the refrigerator? Substitute boar, bear, venison, or beef.

AS GAMEY AS IT GETS

Elk is gamier in flavor than even venison, so keep in mind that the larger the initial flavor, the larger the flavors of the added ingredients.

GRILLED ELK FAJITAS WITH TEQUILA-TOMATILLO SALSA

Wild game is available more and more throughout the country, so if you're making fajitas, why not "get a little wild" and try it with elk? Elk has a wild and gamey flavor in the realm of venison. It's very low in fat, so don't overcook it. As we do in this fun recipe, you want to match the seasoning level and other ingredients to the robustness of the meat. So don't be shy—rub it in, pour it on.

For the home cook, salsas are a wonderful thing. Usually you'll have most of the ingredients on hand, and they can be put together quickly and ahead of time. Salsas are great with grilled meats and fish, and they're also a fantastic way to eat fresh, raw fruits and vegetables. Tart tomatillos are no longer hard to find. Simply remove their papery husks and they're ready to eat.

• SERVES 4 •

ELK MARINADE

2 tablespoons minced garlic

2 teaspoons plus 1 tablespoon vegetable oil

2 teaspoons ground cumin

1½ teaspoons ground coriander

2 teaspoons Creole seasoning, store-bought or homemade (see box, page 9)

½ teaspoon hot or sweet paprika

12 ounces elk backstrap

TEQUILA-TOMATILLO SALSA

5 medium tomatillos (8 to 9 ounces total), chopped

¼ cup fresh lime juice

2 tablespoons gold tequila

1 tablespoon minced shallot

1 tablespoon vegetable oil

2 teaspoons chopped fresh cilantro

2 teaspoons sugar

½ teaspoon ground coriander

¼ teaspoon hot or sweet paprika

¼ teaspoon kosher salt

¼ teaspoon freshly ground black pepper

1 onion, sliced into thick rings

1 medium red bell pepper, halved

1 bunch green onions, trimmed

1 medium jalapeño pepper, halved and seeded

8 flour tortillas, warmed

1 cup grated cheddar or Monterey Jack cheese

1½ tablespoons chopped fresh cilantro

Sour cream

Prepare the elk marinade: In a large bowl, combine the garlic, oil, cumin, coriander, Creole seasoning, and paprika. Add the elk and rub it in the marinade, then let it stand on the counter until the elk is at room temperature. The salsa can be made up to 24 hours ahead.

Prepare the tequila-tomatillo salsa: Place all the ingredients in a medium bowl and stir well to combine. Cover and chill for 1 hour and up to 24 hours.

Prepare a hot fire in a grill.

Remove the elk from the marinade, reserving the marinade, and place the elk on the grill. Grill the elk until an instant-read thermometer registers 130°F when inserted into the thickest part of the meat, about 5 minutes on each side. Transfer the elk to a cutting board and let rest for 5 minutes.

While the elk is grilling, toss the onion, bell pepper, green onions, and jalapeño in the reserved marinade, and add the vegetables to the grill alongside the elk. Grill the vegetables until they are brown all over, 5 minutes total for the jalapeño and green onions, and 8 to 10 minutes total for the onion and bell pepper. Transfer the vegetables to a cutting board. Cut the bell pepper and jalapeño into thin strips. Cut the green onions into 2-inch pieces.

Slice the elk against the grain into thin pieces and serve with the vegetables, salsa, warm tortillas, cheese, cilantro, and sour cream.

TORY'S GAME PLAN

The way to prepare this dish is to first marinate the elk, make the salsa, prepare the grill, and then grill your meat and vegetables. You can even grill your tortillas.

Fried Rabbit Salad with Buttermilk–Black Pepper Dressing

Rabbit has a taste and texture similar to chicken, but it is slightly richer in flavor. Rabbit hunting is big in Louisiana, and you'll find rabbit in many a Southern stew pot. If you haven't been rabbit hunting lately, try this with chicken. This serious salad, loaded with down-home appeal, has been on the lunch menu at Commander's Palace for years now. It is a family favorite. Crusty fried rabbit strips are enhanced by crumbled blue cheese and creamy buttermilk dressing spiked with lots of black pepper.

• SERVES 4 •

1 pound boneless rabbit, cut into 3-inch strips

½ cup dill pickle juice (from the jar)

BUTTERMILK–BLACK PEPPER DRESSING

1 large egg yolk

2 tablespoons buttermilk

1 teaspoon Creole mustard

1 teaspoon fresh lemon juice

¼ teaspoon kosher salt

¼ teaspoon freshly ground black pepper

½ cup vegetable oil

Vegetable oil for frying

1½ cups all-purpose flour

2 tablespoons Creole seasoning, store-bought or homemade (see box, page 9)

1 cup buttermilk

2 heads Bibb lettuce, cut in half, cored, and washed

2 large vine-ripened tomatoes, chopped

1 large cucumber, peeled, halved, seeded, and thinly sliced on the bias

1 small sweet onion, sliced into very thin rings

Salt and freshly ground black pepper

2 teaspoons crumbled blue cheese

Combine the rabbit strips and the pickle juice in a medium nonreactive bowl and marinate in the refrigerator for 1 hour.

Prepare the buttermilk–black pepper dressing: Combine the egg yolk, buttermilk, mustard, lemon juice, salt, and pepper in a blender and process on high speed for 15 seconds. With the motor running, add the oil in a slow, steady stream and process until emulsified. Set aside. (The dressing can be made 3 days ahead; cover and refrigerate.)

Fill a medium pot halfway with oil and heat it to 350°F.

Combine the flour and 1 tablespoon of the Creole seasoning in a medium bowl.

Drain the rabbit strips in a colander, discarding the pickle juice. Return the rabbit to the bowl and add the buttermilk and ½ tablespoon of the Creole seasoning, tossing to combine. In two batches, remove the rabbit from the buttermilk, letting the excess drain away, and toss it in the seasoned flour until the strips are evenly coated and very dry on all sides. Place the rabbit on a large plate.

While maintaining a consistent temperature of 350°F, fry the rabbit in four batches, turning the pieces occasionally, until golden brown and cooked through, 3½ to 4 minutes per batch. Transfer to paper towels to drain and season with Creole seasoning.

In a large bowl, combine the lettuce, tomatoes, cucumber, onion, ¼ cup of the dressing, and salt and pepper to taste. Toss, and divide among four plates. Top with the rabbit. Drizzle the remaining dressing over the salads and sprinkle with the blue cheese.

Rabbit and Goat Cheese Turnovers

A good hunter and a good cook waste nothing. Confit and turnovers are time-honored ways to preserve meat and use leftovers. Confit is a French method for cooking meat or game in its own fat. The process intensifies the flavor and produces meltingly tender meat that shreds with the slight touch of a fork. Here buttery puff pastry envelops creamy goat cheese, herbs, and little pieces of rabbit confit packed with flavor. For a light lunch, serve the turnovers with lightly dressed salad greens. Or make small bite-size turnovers and pass them as hors d'oeuvres at your next party.

• MAKES ABOUT 16 TURNOVERS •

Rabbit Confit

One 2½-pound rabbit, cut into 8 pieces (tenderloin reserved for another use)

1 teaspoon kosher salt

1 teaspoon chopped fresh thyme, plus 1 sprig

½ teaspoon freshly ground black pepper

About 4 cups vegetable oil

3 garlic cloves, crushed

2 bay leaves

½ cup thinly sliced red onion

1 cup thinly sliced cremini mushrooms

4 ounces goat cheese, at room temperature

1 tablespoon chopped fresh thyme

⅛ teaspoon kosher salt

⅛ teaspoon freshly ground black pepper

4 sheets (two 17-ounce packages) frozen prepared puff pastry, thawed

1 large egg, lightly beaten

Prepare the rabbit confit: Place the rabbit pieces in a 9-inch square baking dish and season on all sides with the salt, chopped thyme, and ground pepper. Cover and chill for 8 to 12 hours.

Preheat the oven to 225°F.

Drain off the excess liquid from the rabbit. Add enough oil to the baking dish to cover the rabbit. Add the garlic, bay leaves, and the sprig of thyme. Cover tightly with aluminum foil and cook for 1 hour and 45 minutes, until the meat is tender and falling off the bones.

Transfer the rabbit to a platter and let it cool to room temperature. Discard the bay leaves. Reserve the oil in an airtight container (it will keep in the refrigerator for up to 2 weeks).

Pick the meat from the bones, chopping any large pieces. Cover and refrigerate the meat until ready to use. (The meat will keep, tightly covered and refrigerated, for up to 5 days. Cover it with some of the confit oil if you plan to do this, as the oil will seal out any oxygen.)

Preheat the oven to 400°F.

Heat 2 teaspoons of the reserved confit oil in a medium skillet over medium-high heat. Add the onion and cook, stirring, until translucent, 3 minutes. Add the mushrooms and cook, stirring, until they are soft and give off their liquid, 3 to 4 minutes. Remove the skillet from the heat and stir in the rabbit confit, goat cheese, thyme, salt, and pepper. Stir until the cheese is completely incorporated.

Unfold the pastry sheets on a lightly floured surface and roll with a rolling pin to form a square just a little larger than the original shape. Cut each puff pastry sheet into four squares.

Using your finger or a pastry brush, lightly brush some of the beaten egg around the edges of each pastry square. Place a scant ¼ cup of the filling in the center of each square, and fold the pastry over the filling, pressing the edges together to completely enclose it and form a triangle.

Place the turnovers on a large ungreased baking sheet. Crimp the edges of each pastry with a fork to seal them, and brush the tops with beaten egg. Bake for 15 to 20 minutes, until the pastry is golden brown and crisp and the filling is hot.

Grilled Wild Boar Chops with Southern Comfort–Apricot Glaze

Wild boar are pretty scary beasts. And as if they weren't scary and fast enough, you hunt wild boar in tall grass or heavy trees and brush. You can't see them coming—you only hear them (hopefully!). Southern Comfort would be excellent to have on hand to calm your nerves after the hunt, or to pour into this glaze.

Boar has a flavor of pork, but more intense. One end of a rack of wild boar is larger than the other end, so to ensure even cooking, cut the rack in half and cook each portion separately to the desired temperature.

• SERVES 6 AS A MAIN COURSE, OR 18 AS HORS D'OEUVRES •

SOUTHERN COMFORT–APRICOT
GLAZE

1 cup plus 2 tablespoons Southern
  Comfort
1 cup dried apricots, thinly sliced
1 cup light corn syrup
½ teaspoon crushed red pepper flakes

2 tablespoons vegetable oil
Two 26-ounce wild boar racks (9 ribs
  each), frenched and cut in half
  (see box, page 117)
1 tablespoon Creole seasoning,
  store-bought or homemade
  (see box, page 9)

Prepare the Southern Comfort–apricot glaze: Combine 1 cup Southern Comfort with the apricots, corn syrup, and red pepper flakes in a small skillet and bring to a simmer over medium heat. Simmer, stirring occasionally, until large bubbles form and the mixture is thick and reduced to 1½ cups, 10 minutes. Remove from the heat and stir in the remaining 2 tablespoons Southern Comfort. Keep warm.

Prepare a medium-hot fire in a grill.

Rub the oil into all sides of the boar racks and season with the Creole seasoning. Place the rack halves on the grill, fat side down, and cook over medium-high heat until they are well browned, with good grill marks, and until the fat is starting to crisp (watch for flare-ups as the fat renders from the meat), about 10 minutes. Turn the racks over and cook for about 8 minutes, until an instant-read thermometer inserted into the thickest part of each half registers 130°F for medium-rare. Brush half of the glaze all over the racks and grill for another 30 seconds on each side.

Transfer the racks to a cutting board and cover with aluminum foil to keep warm. Let rest for 10 minutes. Then cut between the bones and partition the racks into separate chops. Arrange the chops decoratively on a platter, and serve the remaining warm glaze on the side for dipping.

No boar? Substitute lamb or pork chops or any type of game.

FRENCHING

When a rack is "frenched," it means that all meat and fat between the ends of the rib bones are trimmed off so that the roasted meat is ready for slicing at the table. Frenching is done for presentation's sake mostly, so you can avoid the step altogether; or ask your butcher to do it for you.

GARLIC AND ROSEMARY–STUDDED
WILD BOAR ROAST

This rosemary-scented preparation is vaguely Italian, with an autumnal touch of pears and apples. It's perfect for a Sunday afternoon with friends. Enjoy any leftovers the next day, mounded onto split chunks of Italian bread and topped with apple chutney. You can also brine the roast in hard apple cider and smoke it over apple wood before starting this recipe.

• SERVES 6 •

One 2½-pound wild boar roast, leg bone removed

2 tablespoons Creole seasoning, store-bought or homemade (see box, page 9)

50 small clusters fresh rosemary leaves (about 1 big bunch)

50 garlic slivers (about 5 heads)

2 tablespoons vegetable oil

Two 8-ounce firm-ripe Bartlett pears, peeled, cored, and quartered

1 cup chopped onions

2 medium apples, peeled, cored, and chopped

½ cup chopped carrots

½ cup chopped celery

½ cup Jack Daniels bourbon

2 cups veal demi-glace (available at gourmet markets)

Preheat the oven to 350°F.

Season the roast inside and outside with the Creole seasoning. Fold the roast over so that it resembles the original shape, as if it still had the bone intact. Cut four long pieces of butcher's twine, and secure the roast's shape by tying it in four places, with the knots on top of the roast. With a sharp paring knife, cut fifty ½-inch-deep slits around the entire roast. Using the tip of the knife, poke the rosemary leaves and a garlic sliver into each slit. Rub the roast on all sides with 1 tablespoon of the oil.

Heat the remaining 1 tablespoon oil in a large ovenproof skillet or Dutch oven over medium-high heat. Add the roast, fat side down, and sear until deep brown, 2½ minutes. Turn the roast over and sear on all sides, 10 minutes total.

Arrange the pears around the meat and roast in the oven for 15 minutes. Turn the roast over and continue cooking for about 30 minutes, until an instant-read thermometer inserted into the thickest part of the meat registers 120°F.

Transfer the roast and pears to a platter, cover with aluminum foil to keep warm, and let rest for 20 minutes.

Heat the same skillet or Dutch oven over medium-high heat until hot. Add the onions, apples, carrots, and celery and cook, stirring constantly to dislodge as much of the brown bits in the pan as possible, until the vegetables are caramelized, about 12 minutes. Remove from the heat and carefully add the Jack Daniels (watch out for a flare-up). Return the pan to the heat and bring to a simmer. Cook until the bourbon is nearly evaporated, 2 minutes. Add the demi-glace and return to a simmer. Cook until it has reduced to a sauce consistency, 5 minutes. Strain the sauce.

Remove the butcher's twine, and using a sharp slicing knife, slice the roast as thin as possible. Serve the roast with the pears, drizzled with the sauce.

No wild boar? Substitute a boneless roast of venison, pork, or lamb (boneless leg).

Buffalo Grillades and Grits

The hunting-fishing-cooking show we had on Turner South for six years captured lots of action and many silly moments. If you ever saw the buffalo episode (no, we didn't kill any—just followed them around on Ted Turner's ranch), you know what we mean. Suffice it to say that Danny Trace, one of our chefs, learned that buffalo can be very friendly and have very long, large tongues. Eeuwh! Do not let this deter you from cooking with this super-lean and flavorful meat. Buffalo is actually a perfect choice for people who are reluctant to try game. It's relatively mild and tastes beefy.

Grillades and grits, a classic New Orleans dish, is usually made with veal and is often served at the Queen's supper after Mardi Gras balls—a good way to absorb all that alcohol.

• SERVES 4 •

GRITS

1 tablespoon unsalted butter

¼ medium onion, diced

2 cups milk

Kosher salt and freshly ground black
  pepper to taste

½ cup stone-ground white grits, rinsed
  (see box, page 121)

½ teaspoon chopped fresh thyme

GRILLADES

1½ pounds buffalo tenderloin, cut into
  ½-inch-thick slices

1½ cups plus 2 tablespoons
  all-purpose flour

1½ teaspoons Creole seasoning,
  store-bought or homemade
  (see box, page 9)

¼ cup vegetable oil

1 cup thinly sliced onions

1 cup thinly sliced green bell peppers

1 cup thinly sliced button mushrooms

½ cup thinly sliced leek (white part
  only), rinsed well

1 teaspoon minced garlic

1 teaspoon tomato paste

1 cup dry red wine

1 cup veal or beef stock

Kosher salt and freshly ground black
  pepper to taste

Prepare the grits: In a medium saucepan, melt the butter over medium heat. Add the onion and cook until translucent (do not brown). Add the milk and bring to a boil. Add the salt, pepper, and grits, whisking constantly until smooth. Reduce the heat and simmer until the grits are tender, about 1½ hours. Add the thyme and adjust the seasoning. Keep hot.

Prepare the grillades: Place the meat between two pieces of plastic wrap on a work surface, and pound with a meat mallet or the bottom of a heavy skillet into ¼-inch-thick slices. Place the 1½ cups flour in a shallow bowl and stir in the Creole seasoning. Dredge the buffalo in the flour mixture, shaking off the excess.

Heat the oil in a large cast-iron skillet or Dutch oven over medium-high heat. Add the buffalo in small batches, and sear until well browned, about 1 minute on each side. Transfer the meat to a platter.

In the same skillet, whisk in the remaining 2 tablespoons flour and cook, stirring constantly, until it's the color of pale peanut butter. Add the onions, bell peppers, mushrooms, leek, and garlic and cook, stirring, over medium-high heat until the vegetables are very soft and starting to color, 4 to 5 minutes. Add the tomato paste and cook, stirring constantly, for 2 minutes. Deglaze the skillet with the wine and reduce until it is almost dry, 10 minutes. Gradually whisk in the stock and bring to a simmer. Skim off any foam (impurities) and cook for 5 minutes. Adjust the seasoning with salt and pepper as needed. Return the buffalo to the skillet and cook to warm through, 4 to 5 minutes. Serve immediately over the hot grits.

No buffalo? Substitute veal or beef.

RINSING GRITS

We use stone-ground grits at Commander's for their rich corn flavor. Rinse them in a bowl under cool running water for a minute or two, squeezing them in your hands to remove any husks, which will then float to the top of the water to be skimmed away. Don't let them sit in the water for long, however, because they will absorb too much water and throw off the ratio between grits and cooking liquid.

Black Bear Bourguignonne

This is a hearty French stew, ideal for a winter night by the fire. Bear is big, and not just in size. It has big flavors that demand big-flavored ingredients. Marinating the bear for 24 hours delivers flavor and tenderizes the meat, as does stewing it in a full-bodied red wine.

• SERVES 4 •

2 pounds boneless black bear meat, cut into ¾-inch cubes

4 cups dry red wine

1 cup chopped garlic

1 onion, julienned

1 medium leek (white part only), cut into thin strips and rinsed well

2 carrots, diced

6 ounces button mushrooms, wiped clean and quartered (about 2 cups)

5 sprigs fresh thyme

2 sprigs fresh oregano

2 teaspoons kosher salt, plus additional to taste

1 teaspoon freshly ground black pepper, plus additional to taste

¼ cup vegetable oil

2 quarts veal or beef stock

Combine the bear, wine, garlic, vegetables, herbs, salt, and pepper in a large bowl and stir well. Cover and refrigerate for 12 to 24 hours.

Drain the meat and vegetables, reserving the liquid. Next, separate the bear meat from the vegetables. Discard the thyme and oregano sprigs.

Add the oil to a large pot or Dutch oven and heat over high heat for 3 minutes, until hot and smoking. Carefully add the meat and sear until it is brown all over, 6 to 8 minutes. Transfer the meat to a bowl.

In the same pot, add the reserved vegetables and cook over high heat until caramelized, about 5 minutes. Deglaze with the reserved wine marinade, 20 minutes. Bring to a simmer and reduce until almost dry. Add the stock and bring to a simmer. Add the bear meat and cook, covered, over low heat, stirring occasionally, until the bear is very tender, 1½ to 2 hours.

With a slotted spoon, transfer the meat and vegetables to a platter. Return the pot to the stove and reduce the sauce over medium heat until it is thickened and shiny, about 15 minutes. Adjust the seasoning with additional salt and black pepper. Return the braised meat and vegetables to the finished sauce, and serve.

No bear? Any other wild game will do here, although classically this dish is made with beef.

CHICKEN FRYIN' MOUNTAIN LION

In Washington and Montana, where Tory's family lives, the state releases a limited number of tags for hunters to hunt mountain lions. This is necessary to control the mountain lion population and to ensure that the wilderness remains in balance. We've never hunted mountain lion, but Tory's family has, and they have shared some of their harvest with us. It's very, very good and considered among connoisseurs to be the best-flavored wild game of all because cats by nature are very finicky and eat only what they kill themselves. This diet is reflected in their flavor.

Wild game doesn't have to be fancy. We admit we love chicken-fried steak, and we've adapted that to mountain lion. It's down-home and darn good.

• SERVES 4 •

1 pound boneless mountain lion cutlets

4 cups plus 2 tablespoons all-purpose flour

3 teaspoons kosher salt, plus additional to taste

1½ teaspoons freshly ground black pepper

6 large eggs

½ cup buttermilk

2 cups vegetable oil

4 ounces breakfast sausage, diced

¼ cup diced onion

1½ cups milk

1 tablespoon Tabasco sauce

2 teaspoons chopped fresh sage

2 teaspoons Worcestershire sauce

Place the cutlets between two pieces of plastic wrap on a work surface, and pound very thin with a meat mallet. In a large bowl, combine the 4 cups flour, 1 teaspoon of the salt, and ½ teaspoon of the black pepper. In another large bowl, whisk together the eggs and buttermilk. Season the cutlets with the remaining 2 teaspoons salt and 1 teaspoon pepper. Dip the cutlets into the egg mixture, letting any excess drip off, and then dredge them in the flour mixture. Then repeat, dipping them in the egg mixture and dredging in the flour so that a thick, very dry crust develops.

Add the oil to a large skillet and heat over medium-high heat for 5 minutes, until hot but not smoking. Add the cutlets, in batches, leaving room around them, and fry until crisp and evenly golden brown, 1 minute on each side. Transfer the cutlets to a platter and keep warm.

Drain off the liquid from the skillet and wipe it clean with a paper towel. Heat the skillet over medium heat for 3 minutes. Add the sausage and onion and cook, stirring occasionally, until the onion is translucent and the sausage is shrunken, 4 minutes. Gradually sprinkle in the remaining 2 tablespoons flour, and stir. Cook until the flour has absorbed all the remaining liquid, 3 minutes. Gradually pour in the milk, stirring constantly to avoid lumps, and bring to a simmer, stirring occasionally. Add the Tabasco, sage, and Worcestershire and reduce the heat to low. Cook for 10 minutes. Adjust the seasoning as necessary, keeping in mind that all sausages are seasoned differently, and some may be saltier or spicier than others.

Place the cutlets on a platter and serve the gravy on the side.

No mountain lion? Substitute beef, veal, pork, alligator, or chicken.

TORY'S WILD GAME SAUSAGE

Don't be intimidated by sausage. You may not have practice making it, but if you follow this recipe you will end up with better-tasting sausage than even the butcher makes. Guaranteed! You don't need any special equipment. You can grind it in a food processor and use plastic wrap as casing instead of natural casings. You can make any game—or honestly, anything—into sausage, but game sausage is especially tasty and is a great way to empty your freezer.

In a classic sausage the mixture is usually one third each of pork, pork fat, and a flavoring meat such as game. If you have a lot of game, you can omit the pork altogether, but you'll need to increase the pork fat (usually bacon) to 40 percent to make up for the leaner meat. One of the secrets of making firm sausage is starting with very cold meat—as cold as you can get without it being frozen (but a little frost is ok).

Sausage needs herbs to help balance the flavor. We use herbes de Provence, which is a dried herb blend popular in the South of France that includes lavender, marjoram, thyme, and oregano; but you can substitute any variety of herbs, depending on your own taste. We find that dried herbs within sausage recipes are more consistent and the flavors are more stable over time than with fresh herbs.

• MAKES ABOUT SIX 11-INCH-LONG SAUSAGES •

1½ pounds game meat, cubed

1½ pounds pork stew meat, cubed

1½ pounds fatty bacon (such as bacon ends and pieces), coarsely chopped

2 tablespoons smoked paprika (available at gourmet markets)

2¼ teaspoons Creole seasoning, store-bought or homemade (see box, page 9), plus additional to taste if necessary

½ teaspoon herbes de Provence or dried thyme

1 teaspoon vegetable oil

Combine all the ingredients except the oil in a medium bowl, and toss. Pass the mixture through a meat grinder fitted with a large die into a medium bowl (if you like a softer texture, run it through twice). Alternatively, process the mixture in a food processor. Mix the meat thoroughly with your hands.

To check the seasoning level of the sausage before you proceed, cook some in a skillet: Heat the oil in a small skillet over medium heat. Form 2 tablespoons of the sausage mixture into a patty and cook until browned, about 2 minutes on each side. Taste the sausage, and then add more Creole seasoning to the un-cooked mixture if desired. A good cook will taste test after each addition of seasoning to ensure the blend is just right.

Lay a large piece of plastic wrap on a work surface with the longer side facing you, and spoon some of the sausage mixture across the center in the shape of a rope. Bring the bottom part of the wrap up and over the mixture, pushing tightly with your hands to form a large cylinder about 2½ inches in diameter and 11 inches long. Roll the sausage in the plastic wrap, pulling the wrap tightly. Twist the ends to tighten them and then fold each end to the center. Wrap the cylinder in a second layer of plastic wrap, twisting the ends to seal. Repeat with the remaining sausage mixture; you should end up with about six sausages.

Place the wrapped sausages in a large roasting pan set over two burners, and add enough cold water to cover them by ½ inch. Rest a medium baking sheet on top of the sausages to weight them down slightly. Cook over low heat until an instant-read thermometer inserted into the center of a sausage reaches 140°F, about 1 hour. (It's crucial that the cooking water not rise above 150°F because if it does, the fat in the sausage will separate from the meat. If the water gets too hot, add a couple of handfuls of ice.) Drain the sausages and transfer them to a deep roasting pan filled with ice water. Let sit for 2 hours to chill.

Drain the chilled sausages, and using scissors, cut away the plastic wrap. To eat immediately, remove the plastic wrap, slice, and serve. If not serving right away, rewrap in clean plastic wrap. (The sausages can be kept in the refrigerator for up to 1 week and frozen for up to 3 months.)

NOT-SO-WILD
GAME

WE COULDN'T EXCLUDE PORK, BEEF, AND LAMB from our cookbook even though we don't hunt them. We love them all, and there's no doubt that this country is still all about meat and potatoes. Beef is king on the grill, but so is a juicy pork tenderloin and flavorful lamb. For special occasions, rib eyes, tenderloin, or lamb chops fit the bill, but if you're cooking for a crowd, surprise your friends and family with the deep flavor of more affordable cuts such as short ribs, flank steak, and leg of lamb.

Lamb prices have gone through the roof. We have always served lamb at Commander's Palace and we will not serve a lower-quality lamb as we fear most restaurants have done due to the steep price increase of Colorado lamb. We most often serve it with the Creole mustard crust, and getting a spoonful of crust that has fallen into the pan can account for many a calorie for us both.

The coffee-crusted pork is so quick and good that it'll make you the star of a dinner party full of foodies.

When it comes to beef, always purchase the best you can afford, especially for steaks, because the cash you spend is directly related to how beefy the taste is.

The top three grades are prime, choice, and select. Prime is the most expensive and the highest quality, meaning it has more marbling and thus more flavor; choice follows with less marbling and less flavor; and finally there's select. Tory discovered a small ranch in California that raises impeccable beef—it's prime, worth every penny, and the only beef we serve at Commander's. Whether you favor steaks cooked outside on the grill or meat so luscious that it falls apart with your fork, these dishes will deliver an exceptionally satisfying feast.

NOT-SO-WILD GAME

COFFEE-CRUSTED PORK LOIN WITH FIG-BOURBON SYRUP

Virtually every Louisianian has a fig tree in their backyard. And every summer without fail, we put up hundreds of jars of fig preserves and find countless uses for them throughout the year. However, if you don't have any preserves, you can still enjoy this pork: Substitute 1 cup sliced dried figs combined with 1 cup water and ½ cup sugar for the preserves. The boozy, sweet fig-bourbon syrup is an excellent foil for the coffee-crusted pork. People rarely consider using coffee as a spice; it's an excellent flavor booster and is almost always hanging out in your cupboard.

• SERVES 8 •

FIG-BOURBON SYRUP

2 cups fig preserves

1 cup bourbon

¼ teaspoon kosher salt

Pinch of freshly ground black pepper

¼ cup finely ground chicory or regular coffee

1 tablespoon plus 2 teaspoons dark brown sugar

1 tablespoon Creole seasoning, store-bought or homemade (see box, page 9)

1 teaspoon smoked paprika (available at gourmet markets)

1 tablespoon vegetable oil

One 2-pound trimmed boneless pork roast, preferably loin

Prepare the fig-bourbon syrup: Combine all the ingredients in a medium saucepan over low heat, and cook, stirring occasionally, for 20 minutes. Keep warm.

Prepare a medium-hot fire in a grill.

Combine the coffee, brown sugar, Creole seasoning, and paprika in a spice grinder and pulse until fine. Rub the oil into the pork and then spread the rub evenly over all sides. Grill the pork, with the grill lid closed, turning it every 5 minutes, for about 20 minutes total, until an instant-read thermometer inserted into the center registers 130°F.

Transfer the pork to a cutting board, cover to keep it warm, and let it rest for 10 minutes. Serve the pork drizzled with the syrup.

LEMON AND GARLIC GRILLED PORK

Pork tenderloin is incredibly versatile and can be cooked in a flash. It makes the perfect midweek meal. It's fairly lean and benefits from time spent in a tasty marinade, not just for flavor, but also for tenderizing. Virtually anything can be added to a marinade as long as it includes an acid such as lemon or lime juice and some seasoning like herbs, garlic, and spices.

If you want to elaborate on the roast, combine plain yogurt with a little minced garlic, chopped cucumber, olive oil, and fresh mint and serve it alongside the pork, along with grilled pita.

• SERVES 4 •

2 lemons, zested, grated, and juiced

1 tablespoon vegetable oil

2 tablespoons minced garlic

2 teaspoons kosher salt

2 teaspoons chopped fresh thyme

1½ teaspoons freshly ground black pepper

1½ pounds boneless pork tenderloin

In a large bowl, whisk together all the ingredients except the pork. Add the pork, turn to coat it with the marinade, and marinate, covered, turning it over occasionally, in the refrigerator for 12 to 24 hours.

Prepare a medium-hot fire in a grill.

Remove the pork from the marinade. Grill the pork for 3½ minutes on each side for medium-rare, or 4½ minutes for medium. Transfer the pork to a plate and let it rest for 5 minutes before slicing.

TORY'S IMPROV

Bring this dish along on your next hunting, fishing, or camping trip: Put the marinade in a self-seal plastic bag, add your pork, jam it in an ice chest, and you're good to go.

BRAISED BEEF SHORT RIBS
WITH SWEET ONIONS

Short ribs taste just as great as rib eye and strip loin (they actually rest against these cuts) but are pretty tough in comparison. Yet through hours of long, slow cooking they become incredibly tender. If you're going to invest 6 hours of cooking time (all thankfully unattended in the oven), start with the best beef possible. At Commander's Palace, we use Harris Ranch beef because it's simply the best-tasting beef in the United States. This small ranch, right outside of Fresno, California, is very strict about quality and breeding. To order, visit their Web site at www.harrisranch.com.

• SERVES 6 •

DRY RUB

6 tablespoons dark brown sugar

2 teaspoons granulated onion

2 teaspoons granulated garlic

2 teaspoons smoked paprika
(available at gourmet markets)

1 teaspoon cayenne pepper

1 teaspoon ground allspice

1 teaspoon Creole seasoning,
store-bought or homemade
(see box, page 9)

1 teaspoon ground cumin

1 teaspoon crushed red pepper flakes

1 teaspoon kosher salt

1 teaspoon freshly ground black pepper

1 teaspoon ground coriander

RIBS

4 pounds boneless beef short ribs, cut
into 6 equal portions

½ cup vegetable oil

6 sweet onions, such as Vidalia, Walla
Walla, Maui, or Texas Sweets:
2 coarsely chopped, 4 halved
lengthwise and sliced thin

4 celery stalks, chopped

2 carrots, chopped

15 garlic cloves

2 cups red wine

3 quarts beef stock or canned
low-sodium beef broth

Prepare the dry rub: Combine all the ingredients in a medium bowl and stir well. (The dry rub can be stored in an airtight container at room temperature for up to 1 month.)

Preheat the oven to 300°F.

Prepare the ribs: Sprinkle at least half of the dry rub over the ribs and use your hands to rub it into the meat. In a large roasting pan set over two burners, heat the oil over high heat until it is hot and just smoking. Add the ribs in batches and sear until very brown on all sides, 10 minutes. Transfer the meat to a platter.

Add the chopped onions, celery, carrots, and garlic to the pan and cook, stirring, until the vegetables are caramelized, 10 minutes. Deglaze the pan with the wine, stirring up any browned bits, and cook until it has almost completely evaporated, about 5 minutes. Add the stock and bring to a simmer. Return the ribs to the pan and bring back to a simmer. Cover the pan, transfer it to the oven, and bake for 2 hours.

Turn the ribs over and bake for 2 more hours.

Stir in the sliced onions and cook for an additional 2½ hours, until the meat is very tender and almost falling apart. Adjust the seasoning with more dry rub or salt and pepper.

CREOLE MUSTARD–CRUSTED RACK OF LAMB WITH MINT JULEP JUS

There is Colorado lamb and then there is everything else. Colorado lamb prices have sky-rocketed but we've stuck with it, and you should too. With every succulent, tasty bite, you'll know your investment was worth it.

We've served lamb many ways, but we always come back to this dish, and we all fight in the kitchen for the little bits of Creole mustard crust that fall off. It's one of the mainstays on the Commander's Palace menu.

Bacon fat may be out of fashion, but it tastes great. You can sear the lamb racks in vegetable oil, but you won't get the same smoky, robust flavor. So next time you're cooking bacon, have a jar ready to save the fat.

• SERVES 4 •

MINT JULEP JUS

½ cup coarsely chopped fresh mint leaves

2 tablespoons sugar

2 tablespoons coarsely chopped shallot

¾ cup bourbon

1 cup veal demi-glace (available at gourmet markets), or 2 cups canned low-sodium beef broth

2 racks of lamb (each with 8 bones), frenched (see box, page 117)

2 teaspoons Creole seasoning, store-bought or homemade (see box, page 9)

6 slices bacon

2 cups fine dry bread crumbs

1 tablespoon chopped fresh rosemary

1 tablespoon chopped fresh thyme

2 teaspoons kosher salt

1 teaspoon freshly ground black pepper

6 tablespoons Creole mustard or other whole-grain mustard

Prepare the mint julep jus: Combine ¼ cup of the mint leaves, the sugar, and the shallot in a small saucepan and mash roughly with the back of a spoon to extract the mint oils. Add the bourbon and bring to a simmer over medium heat. Simmer until the mixture is thick, large bubbles are starting to form on the surface, and it has reduced to about 2 tablespoons, 10 to 12 minutes. Add the demi-glace, return to a simmer, and cook until the sauce is thick enough to coat the back of a spoon, 5 to 10 minutes. (If you are using beef broth, the reducing will take about 25 minutes and the sauce won't have the same body and richness as the demi-glace version.)

Remove the sauce from the heat and stir in the remaining ¼ cup mint leaves. Let steep for 5 minutes. Then strain the mixture through a fine-mesh strainer into a clean saucepan, pressing down on the solids with the back of a spoon. Keep warm.

Preheat the oven to 350°F.

Cut each rack of lamb in half to make four 4-rib half racks. Using a sharp knife, score the fat of each portion in a diamond pattern, being careful not to cut the flesh. Rub each side of each half rack with ½ teaspoon of the Creole seasoning.

In a large skillet, cook the bacon over medium heat until crisp. Transfer the bacon to a plate. Add the lamb racks, fat side down, to the bacon fat in the skillet and sear until they are deep brown and the fat is starting to render, 5 minutes. Turn them over and sear on the remaining sides for 1½ to 2 minutes on each side. Transfer the racks to a work surface and pour half of the pan juices into a large bowl. Add the bread crumbs, rosemary, thyme, salt, and pepper to that bowl and combine well to blend all the ingredients.

Rub the mustard over the lamb meat (not the bones) and add the racks to the bowl with the bread-crumb mixture. Turn to coat them on all sides and press to make the bread crumbs adhere.

Place a rack in a large roasting pan and arrange the lamb on top of it. Roast until medium-rare, 25 to 30 minutes, until an instant-read thermometer inserted into the thickest part of the lamb registers 130°F. Transfer the racks to a platter, cover with aluminum foil to keep them warm, and let rest for 10 to 15 minutes.

Cut each portion in half so that each person gets two double chops, and serve drizzled with the sauce.

GRILLED LAMB AND LENTIL SALAD WITH WARM TASSO VINAIGRETTE

We like our salads with a variety of tastes and textures—we call them composed salads in the Commander's Palace kitchen. Entrée salads are a good place for experimentation and improvisation because just about anything goes. To change things up a bit, we sometimes roast a variety of vegetables, for example, barley or orzo, for this salad and arrange them attractively on the plate alongside the lamb.

• SERVES 4 •

WARM TASSO VINAIGRETTE

4 tablespoons olive oil

¼ cup finely chopped tasso (about 1 ounce) (see box, page 10)

1½ tablespoons finely chopped shallot

1 large jalapeño pepper, seeded and finely chopped

Kosher salt and freshly ground black pepper to taste

1½ cups dry red wine

1 tablespoon chopped fresh thyme

2½ cups chicken stock or canned low-sodium chicken broth

1½ cups diced yellow bell peppers

1 large ripe beefsteak tomato, seeded and diced

1 small red onion, diced

¼ cup red lentils

3 teaspoons Creole seasoning, store-bought or homemade (see box, page 9)

1 pound Colorado boneless lamb loin, trimmed

4 teaspoons vegetable oil

¼ teaspoon kosher salt

¼ teaspoon freshly ground black pepper

6 cups mâche or mesclun (any assortment of fresh salad greens will work here)

Prepare the warm tasso vinaigrette: Heat 2 tablespoons of the oil in a small skillet over medium-high heat. Add the tasso, shallot, jalapeño, salt, and pepper and cook, stirring, until the shallot is caramelized, 2½ minutes. Add the wine, bring to a boil over high heat, and cook until reduced to about ½ cup, 18 to 20 minutes. Transfer the mixture to a bowl. Slowly whisk in the remaining 2 tablespoons oil. Whisk in the thyme and adjust the seasoning to taste. Set aside.

Prepare a medium-hot fire in a grill.

Combine the chicken stock, bell peppers, tomato, red onion, lentils, and ½ teaspoon of the Creole seasoning in a medium saucepan and bring to a simmer over low heat. Cook, uncovered, until the vegetables and lentils are tender, 15 minutes. Drain the lentil mixture and transfer it to a bowl.

Cut the lamb loin in half crosswise to separate the larger from the shorter end (to ensure even cooking). Rub the lamb on all sides with the oil, the remaining 2½ teaspoons Creole seasoning, and season with salt and pepper. Grill until medium-rare, when an instant-read thermometer registers 130°F: about 15 minutes for the smaller loin piece and 20 minutes for the larger piece. Let the lamb rest on a cutting board for 5 minutes, and then slice thin.

Add ¼ cup of the vinaigrette to the lentils and toss. Combine the lettuce and about 1 tablespoon vinaigrette in a bowl, and toss. Divide the greens among the plates and spoon the lentils alongside. Arrange the lamb slices over the greens, and drizzle with the remaining vinaigrette.

CAMPFIRE
COOKING
Easy Cooking Back at Camp

Have you ever picked an ear of corn in the field and eaten it the same day? How about a dripping, juicy bite of a tomato just snipped off the vine and still warm from the sun? These experiences are burned in your brain. That ear of corn and that tomato can never compare to anything store-bought. The same holds true for cooking your day's catch. Food just tastes better when you've worked for it, harvested it, handled it with care, and cooked it yourself.

Soul-satisfying food and the camaraderie of cooking with your friends at camp are the rewards after a day of hunting or fishing. The lure you used today, how you made that Jack Daniels molasses sauce for the duck—where is the rest of that Jack Daniels, by the way—are all bits of conversations you'll overhear. Dinner back at camp has to come together easily and quickly because usually everyone is bone-tired and starving. The dishes in this section are just what the doctor ordered: full-flavored but not fussy. All you really need are your day's catch, a few basic ingredients, a good ol' cast-iron pot or skillet, and a blazing fire.

Grilled Oysters on the Half Shell

You won't believe how delicious these oysters are! Every time we serve them, whether it's back at camp or in our backyard for a neighborhood bash, they are literally devoured. People forget their good manners and hover over the grill, waiting for the next batch. The oysters bubble on the grill in their own juices, then get topped with a lip-smacking garlic-infused butter and a shower of Parmesan. They're salty, briny, smoky, garlicky—frankly the best oysters ever! This recipe makes a dozen, but if you and your friends are as gluttonous as we are, then you'll probably need to double, triple, or even quadruple the recipe. If you really are feeding the neighborhood, buy a whole sack (25 pounds) and shuck and eat them raw until the grill is hot and ready. It will be the one party that everyone talks about until you have your next one.

• MAKES 1 DOZEN OYSTERS •

1 cup (2 sticks) unsalted butter

2 tablespoons minced garlic

2 teaspoons freshly ground black pepper

1 teaspoon dried thyme

1 teaspoon kosher salt

Tabasco sauce to taste

12 oysters on the half shell

½ cup freshly grated Parmigiano-Reggiano cheese

French bread

Prepare a medium-hot fire in a grill.

Melt the butter in a small saucepan over medium heat. Stir in the garlic, pepper, thyme, salt, and Tabasco and cook over low heat for 10 minutes. Spoon half of the garlic butter over the oysters and sprinkle with half of the cheese.

Arrange the oysters on the grill and cook for 2 to 4 minutes, depending on the heat of the grill. Top with the remaining garlic butter and cheese. Serve immediately, with bread.

Shucking live oysters may seem like a hassle, but with just a little practice they open easily, and you can't beat just-shucked for freshness. The two vital parts of shucking are a sturdy oyster knife and caution; you don't want to stab yourself. Working over a bowl to collect the oyster juices, hold the oyster in the palm of a kitchen towel–covered hand. (Some people use a protective rubber mitt, but we find them cumbersome.) Carefully insert the blade of the oyster knife into the gap between the shells at the hinge. Firmly twist the handle of the knife until the hinge pops and separates. Sweep the knife across the inside of the top shell to release the oyster, discard the top shell, and then come back with your knife and run it underneath the oyster to completely free it. Make sure your oysters are free of any tiny shell fragments that occur when shucking.

Dove Poppers with Five-Pepper Jelly

It doesn't take long to figure out that the meal after the hunt is as important as the hunting itself. Once you see the bottles of wine, the jars of secret marinade, the favorite black cast-iron skillet, and the little grills lugged to and unloaded at camp, you know you're in for a serious on-the-spot meal in the awe-inspiring outdoors.

Down here in Louisiana, every hunter we know makes some version of poppers at camp. Our favorite is dove breast rolled around jalapeño slices and jack cheese, then wrapped in bacon, grilled, and dipped in five-pepper jelly. Another version we like is made with duck, has the same fillings, and is fried until hot and crispy. You'll want to make as many of these tasty treats as you can because no one can eat just one—they're addictive, and incredible with a cold beer or a shot of tequila. By the way, they freeze well, too.

• MAKES 24 POPPERS •

12 slices bacon, halved crosswise

24 boneless, skin-on dove breasts (double breasted)

Kosher salt and freshly ground black pepper to taste

2 ounces pepper jack cheese, thinly sliced into strips

3 jalapeño peppers, seeded and thinly sliced into strips

Toothpicks

Five-pepper jelly, or other spicy jelly

Prepare a medium-hot fire in a grill. Preheat the oven to 325°F.

Lay the bacon on a small baking sheet, and bake until it is half-cooked, about 10 minutes. Set the bacon aside until it is cool enough to handle.

Season the dove breasts on both sides with salt and pepper, and place one double breast on each bacon slice, skin side on the bacon. Divide the cheese and jalapeño strips among the dove breasts. Fold each breast over to enclose the filling, and roll the bacon around it. Secure the bacon with a toothpick. (The poppers can be made up to 2 days ahead, covered, and refrigerated; or freeze them for up to 1 month.)

Grill, turning occasionally, for 5 minutes total, until the bacon is crisp. Transfer the poppers to a platter, remove the toothpicks, and let rest for 5 minutes. Serve the poppers with the five-pepper jelly for dipping.

IS THERE A HUNTER IN THE HOUSE?

When butchering wild game birds, always try to leave the skin in place, as it contributes flavor and keeps the lean meat juicy.

WAHOO AND TROPICAL FRUIT SKEWERS WITH COCONUT-RUM DIPPING SAUCE

This is perfect party food: The skewers can be made in advance, as can the dipping sauce. The only step that needs to be done at the last minute is the grilling, which goes quickly.

• SERVES 4 AS A LIGHT LUNCH •

COCONUT-RUM DIPPING SAUCE

¼ cup sugar

1 large egg

3 tablespoons fresh lime juice

3 tablespoons dark rum

2 teaspoons chopped fresh cilantro

2 teaspoons minced shallot

1 teaspoon grated fresh ginger

¼ teaspoon kosher salt

Pinch of crushed red pepper flakes

Pinch of freshly ground black pepper

½ cup unsweetened coconut milk

½ cup vegetable oil

SKEWERS

12 ounces wahoo, cut into 1-inch cubes

2 tablespoons plus 1 teaspoon vegetable oil

½ teaspoon Creole seasoning, store-bought or homemade (see box, page 9)

2 red bell peppers, cut into 1-inch pieces

1 medium red onion, quartered and layers separated

½ pineapple, peeled, trimmed, and cut into cubes

2 mangos, peeled, seeded, and cut into cubes

Four 12-inch metal or wood skewers

Prepare the coconut-rum dipping sauce: In a blender, combine the sugar, egg, lime juice, rum, cilantro, shallot, ginger, salt, red pepper flakes, and black pepper and process until foamy and light in color, 20 seconds. With the motor running, add the coconut milk and the oil and process until emulsified. (The dipping sauce can be made up to 2 days ahead, covered and refrigerated.)

Prepare a medium-hot fire in a grill.

Prepare the skewers: Place the wahoo in a bowl and drizzle the 1 teaspoon oil over it; rub it in. Add the Creole seasoning and toss to coat thoroughly. Alternately thread the wahoo cubes, bell peppers, red onion, and fruit onto the skewers.

(The skewers can be assembled up to 1 day ahead, covered and refrigerated.) Brush the remaining 2 tablespoons oil over the skewers.

Grill, covered, turning the skewers every 2 minutes, for 8 minutes total. Transfer the skewers to a platter and brush with some of the dipping sauce. Serve extra dipping sauce alongside.

Quick Black Skillet Shrimp

If you're cold and hungry and need to eat as soon as you get back to camp, then this recipe is the one. These few ingredients are probably already in the refrigerator, and they require only about 10 minutes to put together, but they deliver big *flavor. Make extra because we guarantee that people are going to line up for seconds. After you taste these shrimp, you'll agree that garlic, lemon, and parsley are a natural match.*

• SERVES 4 AS A FIRST COURSE •

1 pound large shrimp, peeled and deveined

1 teaspoon Creole seasoning, store-bought or homemade (see box, page 9)

12 tablespoons (1½ sticks) cold unsalted butter, cut into pieces

3 tablespoons minced garlic

3½ tablespoons fresh lemon juice (about 4 lemons)

2 tablespoons minced fresh parsley

Four ¾-inch-thick slices French bread (cut on the bias), toasted

Season the shrimp with the Creole seasoning. Heat a large cast-iron skillet over high heat until it is hot but not smoking, 3 minutes. Add the butter. When it has melted, add the garlic and cook, stirring constantly, until golden brown, 1 minute. Add the shrimp, and stirring constantly to prevent the garlic from sticking to the bottom of the skillet, cook until pink, about 3 minutes. Remove the skillet from the heat and stir in the lemon juice and parsley. Serve the shrimp spooned over the bread.

YOUR MAMA'S SKILLET

Seasoned cast-iron skillets are so treasured in the South that they are passed down from generation to generation. If you're not lucky enough to have one of those well-worn beauties, then you will need to season a new skillet before you cook with it. First, rub the skillet or pot (and any lid) inside and out with canola or vegetable oil. Then heat the oiled skillet or pot in a 400°F oven to get it very hot. Remove it from the oven, rub in some coarse salt with a towel (as if you were using sandpaper), wipe the salt out, and let the pan cool. Coat the pan with a thin layer of oil, reheat it until the oil smokes, wipe the pan out, and let it cool again. Never wash the pan with soap and water, and never scour it with steel wool.

GRILLED SHRIMP AND ANDOUILLE SKEWERS WITH SPICY BOURBON MUSTARD

Andouille is a spicy Louisiana smoked sausage that imparts a hint of smokiness to the skewers, whether they're cooked outside on the grill or inside in a pan.

• SERVES 4 •

SPICY BOURBON MUSTARD

¼ cup Creole mustard or other whole-grain spicy mustard

¼ cup honey

2 tablespoons Jack Daniels bourbon or other bourbon

1 teaspoon Chipotle Tabasco sauce

1 pound large shrimp, peeled and deveined, with tails left on

12 ounces andouille or other hot sausage, sliced into ¾-inch-thick rounds

Eight 6-inch sugarcane or bamboo skewers (soak bamboo skewers in water for 30 minutes before using)

2 tablespoons plus ½ teaspoon vegetable oil

1 teaspoon Creole seasoning, store-bought or homemade (see box, page 9)

Prepare the spicy bourbon mustard: Combine all the ingredients in a medium bowl. (The mustard will keep in an airtight container, refrigerated, for up to 1 week.)

Prepare a medium-hot fire in a grill.

Alternately thread the shrimp and sausage rounds onto the skewers (we sometimes thread the shrimp around the andouille like a pinwheel). Rub both sides with the oil, and season with the Creole seasoning. Place the skewers on the grill and cook until the shrimp are pink and cooked through and the sausages are browned and hot all the way through, 2 minutes on each side. During the last 30 seconds of cooking, baste the shrimp with the bourbon mustard. Serve immediately, passing additional spicy mustard on the side.

Left: Hot boiled Louisiana crawfish . . . awaiting company. Below: Orange-Brined Turkey Breast with Spicy Citrus Compote

Above: Truffled Scal-
lops with Crabmeat and
Caviar Vinaigrette
Right: Sighting the guns
before the hunt . . .

Right: . . . Ti and Lally just blowing in the wind. Below: Porch sitting on the way to the bait shack on the way to the hunt. Bottom: Boudin & crawfish & cracklins . . . Oh my . . .

Top: Scenes behind the scene . . .
Above: Where jazz brunch was invented . . . as festive as ever
Right: Grilled Wild Boar Chops with Southern Comfort Apricot Glaze

Above: Creole Cream Cheese Gnocchi with Crawfish
Right: For Tory, it does not get any better . . .

Right: Seared Duck with
Autumn Mushrooms
Below: True Louisiana
sportsmen, enjoying some
time in the deer stand
Bottom: . . . the band always
plays one for the team . . .

*Above: The start of Crawfish Alfredo
Right: In the Zone, plating buttermilk fried rabbit salad*

Above: Crawfish Alfredo! A quick recipe back at the camp
Left: . . . oyster roast . . . favorite shades . . . life is good.

CRACKLIN'-CRUSTED
SOFT-SHELL CRABS

At Commander's Palace, we love soft-shells and buy as many as possible every day when they're in season during the spring and summer. After much experimentation, we believe the best way to enjoy them is fried—they're hot, crunchy, salty, and so plump and juicy that when you bite into the middle they burst with crab flavor.

We got the idea for cracklin'-crusted crabs from our dear friend and Commander's Palace alum John Currence, who is chef/owner of the City Grocery in Oxford, Mississippi. We always have duck on the menu, and consequently make duck cracklin's for garnishes and sous-chef snacks.

To make duck cracklin's at home, remove the skin (with its fat layer), place it in a pot, cover with a little water, and cook over medium heat for about 45 minutes. At that time the water will have evaporated and the cracklin's will start to fry in their own fat. Continue to fry them until they're golden brown and crisp, 15 to 30 minutes. If you don't want to bother with making cracklin's, you can always buy them or substitute crispy pork rinds.

• SERVES 4 •

Canola oil for frying
½ cup milk
2 large eggs
1 cup fine dry bread crumbs or panko
1 cup crushed cracklin's
1 cup all-purpose flour

2 teaspoons Creole seasoning, store-bought or homemade (see box, page 9)
4 large soft-shell crabs (each about 6 inches wide), cleaned (see box, page 53)
Lemon wedges

Heat 2 inches of oil in a large pot to 350°F.

Whisk the milk and eggs together in a medium bowl. In a large bowl, combine the bread crumbs and cracklin's. Place the flour in another large bowl. Divide the Creole seasoning among all three bowls. Dredge the crabs, one at a time, in the flour, being sure to coat them well and evenly even under the flaps that cover the gills. Then dip the crabs in the egg mixture, coating them well and evenly, and dredge them in the bread-crumb mixture, again coating well and evenly. Transfer the crabs to a baking sheet.

Fry the crabs, in two batches, until golden brown and crisp, about 3 minutes. Be sure to let the oil return to 350°F between batches. Serve the crabs with the lemon wedges.

Fried Speckled Trout Po'boys
with Creole Tartar Sauce

Ti says her last meal will be an oyster po'boy, dressed. But this one would be in the running for Tory. When Tory is out fishing, dreams of this po'boy dance through his head.

There are multiple key factors in making this sandwich sublime: fresh speckled trout, crisp New Orleans French bread, this homemade tartar sauce, and knowing the art of lightly frying. If your oil is the proper temperature, you should remove the fish as soon as you hear the hissing stop. As long as you hear hissing, steam is coming out and oil can't get in. Once the hissing stops, oil has begun to penetrate and if you leave the fish in, you will have greasy fillets.

• SERVES 4 •

CREOLE TARTAR SAUCE

1 cup mayonnaise

½ cup chopped green onions
(green part only)

2 tablespoons chopped pickled okra

2 tablespoons chopped capers

1 tablespoon fresh lemon juice

1 teaspoon Tabasco sauce

PO'BOYS

Vegetable oil for frying

One 30-inch loaf French or Italian
bread, ends trimmed, cut in half
lengthwise

Four 6- to 8-ounce trout fillets, skin off

3 tablespoons plus 2¼ teaspoons Creole
seasoning, store-bought or
homemade (see box, page 9)

½ cup Creole mustard or other mild
whole-grain mustard

½ cup milk

3 cups yellow cornmeal

2 ounces arugula or mesclun (1½ cups)

One 12-ounce Creole tomato or other
heirloom tomato, sliced thin

Prepare the Creole tartar sauce: Whisk all the ingredients together in a bowl. (This can be made up to 3 days ahead, covered, and refrigerated.)

Fill a large pot halfway with oil, and heat it to 350°F.

Cut the French bread crosswise into four equal pieces, and split them open. Season the fish on both sides with 2 teaspoons of the Creole seasoning.

Whisk the mustard and milk together in a large bowl. In another large bowl, stir together the cornmeal and the 3 tablespoons Creole seasoning. Dip the fish, 1 fillet at a time, into the mustard mixture to coat well, and then dredge them in the seasoned cornmeal, pressing it down to make sure the coating is uniform and dry.

Fry the fish, in two batches, until golden brown, 2 to 3 minutes. Drain on paper towels. Season the fillets with the remaining ¼ teaspoon Creole seasoning.

Spread the Creole tartar sauce on the bread and top with the arugula, tomato slices, and trout fillets.

No speckled trout? Substitute virtually any white-fleshed fish.

Spicy Crawfish and Avocado Quesadillas

Here in Louisiana we're spoiled with an incredible variety of seafood. Crawfish tails are the perfect Louisiana convenience food because they're already peeled and cooked and need only to be heated up. Sautéed crawfish, plenty of tomatoes and green onions, a bit of cilantro, some spicy jack cheese, and a squeeze of zesty lime make these quesadillas exciting beyond the sum of their parts.

• MAKES 16 PIECES; SERVES 4 •

2 tablespoons vegetable oil, plus additional for brushing

½ onion, diced

1 tablespoon minced garlic

1 pound cooked Louisiana crawfish tails

1 tablespoon Creole seasoning, store-bought or homemade (see box, page 9)

2 bunches green onions (green part only), sliced thin

1 large tomato, diced

8 flour tortillas

1 pound pepper jack cheese, grated

2 avocados

2 limes, halved

½ cup chopped fresh cilantro

Kosher salt and freshly ground black pepper to taste

Heat a cast-iron skillet over medium-high heat until it is hot but not smoking, 3 minutes. Add the 2 tablespoons oil and swirl to coat the bottom of the skillet. Add the onion and garlic, and cook until just caramelized, 2 minutes. Add the crawfish and Creole seasoning, and cook for 4 minutes. Stir in the green onions and tomato, and remove the skillet from the heat.

Preheat the oven to 350°F.

Brush both sides of the tortillas with a little oil and arrange 4 on a baking sheet. Divide the crawfish mixture and half of the cheese among the tortillas. Slice the avocados and arrange them on top. Squeeze the limes all over, and top with the cilantro, salt, pepper, and remaining cheese. Top with the remaining 4 tortillas and bake for 8 to 10 minutes, until the tortillas are brown and the cheese has melted. Cut into quarters, and serve.

No crawfish? Substitute peeled raw shrimp.

CRAWFISH BOIL

The crawfish boil is a true Louisiana party. Always cooked outside for a large crew, mounds of spicy crawfish, corn, and potatoes are heaped onto a newspaper-lined table, and everyone just digs in. This is a messy business—you have to peel and eat the crawfish with your fingers, and don't forget about sucking their heads, where all the warm, spicy juices are. Peel the tails by pinching the very end and letting the crawfish pop out. Serious locals can devour 5 to 8 pounds of crawfish each!

Did you know that Tory holds the Guinness World Record for the largest crawfish boil in history? He drove to Savannah, Georgia, with three of his good buddies and over 1,000 pounds of food and fired up twenty 80-quart crawfish boil pots to put on a party with Paula Dean. The cooked crawfish spanned twelve picnic tables, stretching over 96 feet, and was documented by the Food Network.

• SERVES 12 •

1 sack (40 to 45 pounds) live crawfish

8 cups salt

6 cups Creole seasoning, store-bought or homemade (see box, page 9)

2 cups cayenne pepper

2 cups whole black peppercorns

12 lemons, halved

15 bay leaves

12 heads garlic, each head cut in half

10 onions, quartered

3 pounds small new potatoes, scrubbed, skin on

12 ears corn, shucked and cut in half

Fill a washtub or ice chest with water and stir in 2 cups of the salt. Add the crawfish. As they swim around, the salt will cause them to purge themselves of impurities and will cleanse their outer shells. Let them purge for 30 to 40 minutes; they need to stay alive until you're ready to cook them.

Meanwhile, pour 12 gallons of water into a 20-gallon pot, and bring to a boil. Add the remaining 6 cups salt and the Creole seasoning, cayenne, peppercorns, lemons, and bay leaves. Boil for 15 minutes. In a basket insert, place half the garlic, half the onions, and half the potatoes and cook for 20 minutes. Add half the corn to the basket and return the water to a boil.

Drain the crawfish, add half of them to the basket, and bring to a rolling boil for 5 minutes. Turn off the heat and let soak for 10 minutes. Then pull out the basket, drain, and dump the basket's contents onto a newspaper-lined table. Repeat with the remaining garlic, onions, potatoes, corn, and crawfish.

CRAWFISH BOILING BASICS

Be sure to have a large pot, at least 20 gallons, with a basket and a lid (the lid helps the liquid to come to a boil faster). You'll probably use a propane tank, so be sure to have enough fuel. Also, place the pot on the burner before you add the water or it will be too heavy to lift. Every cook personalizes his or her boils in different ways—some add andouille sausage, artichokes, or mushrooms. Whatever you do, be sure to have lots of cold beer and other beverages on hand—after eating pounds of crawfish, your lips start to burn.

SWAMP GUMBO

We named this gumbo for the swamp both because the soup looks a little murky and because it combines many of the ingredients found there, such as wild mushrooms and duck. A fancied-up version of this gumbo, which included rabbit, venison, wild boar sausage, and duck (with a homemade popcorn rice and filé cracker), won the 2007 United Way Gumbo Cook-Off in the exotic category.

• MAKES 4 QUARTS; SERVES 16 •

¾ cup rendered duck fat or vegetable oil

1¼ cups all-purpose flour

8 ounces andouille sausage, diced

1 onion, diced

1 green bell pepper, diced

4 celery stalks, diced

½ cup minced garlic

3 tablespoons Creole seasoning, store-bought or homemade (see box, page 9)

1 tablespoon kosher salt

3 bay leaves

3 quarts chicken stock or canned low-sodium chicken broth

2 cups chopped cooked duck meat

8 ounces assorted wild mushrooms, wiped clean and chopped

2 tomatoes, chopped

2 bunches green onions (green part only), sliced thin

In a large pot or Dutch oven, heat the duck fat over high heat until it is hot and just smoking. Gradually whisk in the flour and cook, whisking constantly, until the roux becomes a deep chocolate color, about 10 minutes. Add the andouille, onion, bell pepper, celery, garlic, Creole seasoning, salt, and bay leaves, and sauté for 5 minutes.

Gradually whisk in the stock (to prevent lumps) and bring to a simmer. Simmer for at least 1 hour, stirring occasionally and skimming off any fat that floats to the top. Add the duck, mushrooms, and tomatoes and cook for 5 minutes. Remove and discard the bay leaves. Adjust the seasoning, and garnish with the green onions just before serving.

WILD SEAFOOD STEW IN
BLOODY MARY BROTH

Camp wouldn't be the same without a round of lively Bloody Marys before we make our way out into the wild. And we usually catch a lot of fish out there, so we combined the two in this zesty stew. We make our own Bloody Mary mix at Commander's Palace, but the process is lengthy and time-consuming. For that reason, we recommend a good-quality store-bought variety, such as Tabasco or Zing Zang.

If you prep the vegetables ahead of time and bring them along on your next hunting or fishing trip, this stew will be so easy that you can even pull it off on the boat. How can you beat that for fresh? Watching Tory's face, after catching and cleaning fish on the boat and then eating it within minutes, is like watching a little kid find all his favorite toys under the Christmas tree. His idea of heaven!

• MAKES 3½ QUARTS; SERVES 8 TO 12 •

4 tablespoons (½ stick) unsalted butter

2 tablespoons minced garlic

1 cup finely chopped onions

1 cup finely chopped celery

1 cup finely chopped carrots

1 cup finely chopped leeks (white part only), rinsed well

2 teaspoons Creole seasoning, store-bought or homemade (see box, page 9)

1 quart Bloody Mary mix

2 cups seafood stock or water

2 cups seeded and diced tomatoes

1½ pounds assorted fish fillets, such as redfish, speckled trout, drum, sheepshead, or any other delicate whitefish

8 ounces medium shrimp, peeled and deveined

1 pound jumbo lump or lump crabmeat, picked over for shells and cartilage

2 teaspoons chopped fresh basil

2 teaspoons chopped fresh thyme

Kosher salt and freshly ground black pepper to taste

1 large loaf French bread and/or cooked rice, optional

Melt the butter in a large saucepan over high heat. Add the garlic and cook, stirring, until fragrant, 20 seconds. Add the onions, celery, carrots, leeks, and Creole seasoning and cook, stirring, for 2 minutes. Add the Bloody Mary mix, stock, and tomatoes and bring to a boil. Reduce the heat and simmer, uncovered, for 10 minutes.

Add the fish and shrimp, and cook until the fish just about flakes apart and the shrimp are pink, 1½ to 2 minutes. Stir in the crabmeat and herbs, and cook until the crabmeat is heated through, 1 to 2 minutes. Remove the pan from the heat and adjust the seasoning with salt and pepper. Serve the stew with bread and/or rice, if desired.

BRAISED DUCK AND WILD MUSHROOMS

This succulent stew lends itself to cooking back at camp because all you need is a fire and a heavy cast-iron pot. Braising, or slow cooking in liquid, is a great preparation for tougher meats like duck or wild goose. Eat this with potato cakes, buttered noodles, or mashed potatoes, and pass some crusty bread to mop up all the luscious sauce.

• SERVES 4 •

2 whole ducks (about 4 pounds each), quartered

2 teaspoons kosher salt, plus additional to taste

1 teaspoon freshly ground black pepper, plus additional to taste

4 tablespoons vegetable oil

1 cup diced bacon (about 4 ounces)

1½ cups diced onions

½ cup diced carrots

½ cup diced celery

3 bay leaves

2 teaspoons minced garlic

2 cups cubed assorted mushrooms, such as portobello, cremini, and button, wiped clean and stems trimmed (¾-inch cubes)

1 cup dry red wine

3 cups duck or chicken stock, or canned low-sodium chicken broth

1 teaspoon minced fresh thyme

2 tablespoons unsalted butter, cut into pieces

Preheat the oven to 350°F.

Season the duck on both sides with the salt and pepper. Heat 2 tablespoons of the oil in a large Dutch oven over high heat. Add half of the duck, skin side down, and sear until deep golden brown, 4 to 5 minutes. Turn the duck over and sear the other side. Transfer the duck to a plate. Add the remaining 2 tablespoons oil to the Dutch oven, heat it, and sear the remaining duck. Transfer it to the plate.

Pour off all but 1 tablespoon of the fat from the pan. Reduce the heat to medium-high, add the bacon, and cook until the bacon begins to render some of its fat and is slightly browned, 3 to 5 minutes.

Add the onions, carrots, celery, and bay leaves and cook, stirring occasionally, until the vegetables begin to caramelize, 8 to 10 minutes. Stir in the garlic and cook for 2 minutes. Stir in the mushrooms and cook until they are just soft, 2½ to 3 minutes. Add the red wine and reduce until the liquid is almost completely evaporated, 5 to 6 minutes. Add the duck and the stock, and bring to a simmer.

Cover the pan, transfer it to the oven, and braise for 1 hour. Turn the duck over and braise, covered, for 45 minutes, or until it is tender (time varies depending on size of duck). Transfer the duck to a platter and keep warm.

Transfer the pan with the braising liquid to the stove and bring it to a simmer over medium heat. Cook, skimming off any fat that rises to the surface, until reduced by about a quarter, 20 minutes. Strain the braising liquid into a small saucepan, and swirl in the thyme and butter until melted. Adjust the seasoning with salt and pepper. Serve the duck topped with the sauce.

Smoked Goose and Andouille Jambalaya

Jambalaya is a true one-pot wonder: It has rice, meat, and vegetables all in one. It's stick-to-your-ribs food that everyone in New Orleans cooks up for Mardi Gras parties. There are two camps of jambalaya—one adds tomato and the other balks at the very notion. We like it both ways. Tory judged a jambalaya cook-off for celebrity chef Bobby Flay's Food Network show Throwdown! *Bobby's jambalaya lost that day, so we'll be sending him a copy of this recipe—it's our favorite, and a winner.*

• SERVES 8 •

4 tablespoons (½ stick) unsalted butter

One 3-pound smoked goose, meat removed and chopped (see box, page 162)

1 pound andouille sausage, cut into ¼-inch-thick slices

2 onions, chopped

2 green bell peppers, chopped

20 garlic cloves, minced

3 celery stalks, diced

2 bay leaves

3½ tablespoons Creole seasoning, store-bought or homemade (see box, page 9)

6 cups chicken stock, smoked goose stock, or water

2 tomatoes, peeled, seeded, and diced

Kosher salt and freshly ground black pepper to taste

Tabasco sauce to taste

3 cups long-grain white rice, rinsed thoroughly

2 bunches green onions (green part only), sliced thin

In a large heavy pot or Dutch oven, melt the butter over medium-high heat. Add the goose meat, andouille, onions, bell peppers, garlic, celery, bay leaves, and 1½ tablespoons of the Creole seasoning. Cook until the vegetables are caramelized and a brown crust has developed on the bottom of the pot, 10 minutes. Add the stock, tomatoes, remaining 2 tablespoons Creole seasoning, salt, pepper, and Tabasco. Bring to a boil, scraping up the browned bits on the bottom of the pan. (This flavors the liquid, which is the key to a flavorful jambalaya. The liquid should taste well seasoned, but not overly salty or too spicy. If seasoning is added later, after the rice is cooked, then the rice will taste flat, not deep and rich. The rice will not have had the opportunity to soak up the flavorful liquid as it cooks.)

Stir in the rice and reduce the heat to low. Cover the pot and cook, stirring halfway through, until the rice is tender and all the liquid has been absorbed, 15 to 20 minutes. Remove and discard the bay leaves. Garnish with the green onions.

IS THERE A HUNTER IN THE HOUSE?

If you're bored with roast goose, try smoking it. You don't need any extra equipment—simply fire up your charcoal or gas grill. When the grill is hot, open the grate and add soaked wood chips. Turn the fire down if using a gas grill, add your seasoned goose, and let it cook with the cover on for 1 hour, or until cooked through. Once it is cool, pull off the cooked meat, discarding the fat and skin and saving the bones. To add extra flavor to your stock, smoke the bones again on their own before adding them to your stockpot.

FRIED TURKEY

There's no Thanksgiving bird as moist and flavorful as a fried turkey. We don't just save it for the holidays, though; we often fry them back at camp because it's so much fun and very communal. The key is to know what you're doing, so please read the box for more details.

• SERVES 10 •

1 turkey (about 15 pounds)
3 to 5 gallons vegetable oil
2 tablespoons kosher salt

1 tablespoon freshly ground black pepper

Let the turkey sit at room temperature for 1 hour before frying (this allows it to cook more evenly).

Heat the oil in a turkey fryer to 350°F. Pat the turkey dry with paper towels. Season the turkey with the salt and pepper. Submerge the turkey in the oil and fry until an instant-read thermometer inserted into the thickest part of the thigh registers 155°F, 45 minutes. Remove the turkey from the oil and let it rest for 15 minutes. Serve sliced on its own or with all the Thanksgiving trimmings.

FRYING TURKEY LIKE A PRO

For safety's sake, it's critical to know what you're doing before you attempt to fry a turkey, and to be prepared. First, invest in a real turkey fryer with a fry basket, a handle to get the turkey in and out, and a long-stemmed thermometer. *Whatever you do, don't try this at home on top of the stove.* Fry outside, never inside, always away from people and pets, and ideally on a non-flammable surface. Have everything at the ready: all the frying equipment, a baking sheet to hold the fried turkey, rags for spills, oven mitts, and a fire extinguisher just in case. Use only the amount of oil recommended by the fryer manufacturer. Do not add more than recommended because the hot oil will overflow—not good. Don't run off to do something else—stand by your bird. It should take no more than 1 hour. And finally, save the original oil containers for disposing of or saving the cooled used oil.

SHOWSTOPPING DISHES TO IMPRESS YOUR FRIENDS

OUTHERNERS ARE KNOWN FOR ENTERTAINING LAVISHLY and with ease. They pull off dinner for twelve to fifty and have fun to boot. They make it all look effortless. How do they do this? The key to their success (along with a stiff drink) is serving several dishes that can be prepared in advance. This eases party-day stress and allows one to actually be present at the party. They also usually stick to the dishes they know and maybe mix in one or two new, exciting creations. These are those dishes. Some are favorites at Commander's Palace, but you don't need a kitchen staff to prepare them. All that's required is time, some fancy ingredients, and Chef Tory's precise instructions, and you're set. These dishes have the power to please, and they will certainly spoil your friends.

SHOWSTOPPING DISHES TO IMPRESS YOUR FRIENDS

Truffled Scallops and Crabmeat with Caviar Vinaigrette

Tory could eat this dish every day of his life and never get tired of it. It is the ultimate in luxury, so save it for a special dinner when you want to impress someone. You will have them eating out of your hands with one bite.

• SERVES 4 AS A FIRST COURSE •

8 large dry-pack sea scallops (about 12 ounces total), patted dry with kitchen towels

1½ teaspoons kosher salt, plus an additional pinch

1 teaspoon ground white pepper, plus an additional pinch

4 tablespoons olive oil

½ cup dry white wine

2 tablespoons minced shallots

2 tablespoons unsalted butter

8 ounces jumbo lump crabmeat, picked over for shells and cartilage

1 tablespoon minced fresh chives

1 tablespoon cane vinegar or apple cider vinegar

1 tablespoon white truffle oil

2 teaspoons domestic caviar, such as choupique (bowfin)

Half a recipe Roasted Beet Salad (page 188)

Season the scallops with ½ teaspoon of the salt and ½ teaspoon of the white pepper. Heat 1 tablespoon of the oil in a medium nonstick skillet over medium-high heat until it is hot but not smoking. Add the scallops, in two batches, and sear for about 1 minute on each side. Transfer the scallops to a plate and keep warm.

Add the wine, 1 tablespoon of the shallots, and the butter to the skillet and cook, stirring occasionally, until reduced by half, about 2 minutes. Add the crabmeat, chives, 1 teaspoon salt, and ½ teaspoon white pepper. Cook until just warmed through, being careful not to break up the crabmeat, 1 minute. Keep warm.

In a medium bowl, whisk the remaining 3 tablespoons olive oil with the vinegar, truffle oil, remaining 1 tablespoon shallots, and remaining pinch of salt and white pepper. Gently whisk in the caviar.

To serve, arrange 4 beet slices in the center of each of four small plates and drizzle lightly with the caviar vinaigrette. Place 2 scallops over the beets, and top with the crabmeat mixture. Drizzle a little vinaigrette on top of the crabmeat, and the remaining vinaigrette around each plate.

SCALLOP SENSE

Most scallops are treated with a phosphate solution for preservation purposes and to plump them up. But the problem with that is they ooze so much liquid that you can't get a good sear on them. Spend a little extra and ask for dry-pack scallops—they will be the cream-colored scallops as opposed to the super-white plumped variety. To get a really deep, golden brown sear on the outside and a medium-rare center, have your skillet hot and don't forget to pat the scallops very dry with kitchen towels before seasoning and searing.

CREOLE LOBSTER BISQUE

Lobster season in Florida is short-lived—only a few days a year. You capture these beauties by holding your breath and free-diving for them. Spiny Florida lobsters are leaner, tougher, and chewier than their Yankee relations and can't survive outside water. If you can't find whole Florida lobsters, purchase whole Maine lobsters instead because you need the lobster head to flavor the stock. The recipe may seem long, but most of it has to do with the details of making a flavorful lobster stock, and it's not complicated at all. And besides, the effort is well worth it for the voluptuous result.

• MAKES ABOUT 6 CUPS; SERVES 4 AS A FIRST COURSE •

LOBSTER STOCK

Two 1½-pound lobsters

1 large onion, coarsely chopped

1 large carrot, coarsely chopped

2 celery stalks, coarsely chopped

½ cup dry white wine

3 bay leaves

8 whole black peppercorns

½ cup vegetable oil

½ cup all-purpose flour

4 tablespoons (½ stick) unsalted butter

2 cups coarsely chopped tomatoes
(about 1 pound)

4 shallots, chopped

1 leek (white part only), chopped and
rinsed well

1 celery stalk, chopped

1 small green bell pepper, chopped

1 tablespoon Creole seasoning,
store-bought or homemade
(see box, page 9)

⅓ cup plus a splash of Armagnac or
brandy

¼ cup heavy cream

1 teaspoon chopped fresh thyme

Kosher salt and freshly ground black
pepper

STOCK TIP

The key to flavorful lobster stock is roasting the shells and then breaking them into small pieces so that they have more contact with the water and consequently release more flavor. Another critical step is not to use more water than is necessary—you want a flavorful, intense stock, not watered-down murky muck. And one more thing: Stock should never boil, whether it is chicken, veal, or seafood, because boiling will make the stock cloudy and bitter.

Preheat the oven to 350°F.

Prepare the lobsters: Prepare a large bowl of salted ice water, and set it aside. Bring a large stockpot of salted water (taste it; it should be salty like the sea) to a boil. Add the lobsters and cook over high heat until they are cooked just about halfway through (the lobster cooks again at the end), 4½ minutes. Transfer the lobsters to the ice water to stop the cooking, and let them rest in the water for 4½ minutes.

Holding a lobster over a large bowl, firmly grip the head and the tail with your hands and twist and pull the tail away from the head/body. Repeat with the second lobster. Remove the lobster meat from the shells. Chop the meat and set it aside in a bowl. Place the empty shells in the bowl with the lobster juices. Holding onto the head of the lobster, pull up on the top portion of the shell and pull it away, revealing the gills. Remove and discard the gills. Place the heads and all other lobster shells in the bowl with the lobster juices.

Arrange the coarsely chopped onion, carrot, and celery in a shallow roasting pan. Place the lobster shells on top (do not use the liquid in the bowl), and roast for 20 minutes, until the lobster shells are pale red and the vegetables are starting to caramelize.

Remove the pan from the oven and transfer the ingredients to a standing mixer fitted with the paddle attachment. Wrap the mixer with a kitchen towel (to prevent the lobster shells from flying out) and mix for about 1 minute on low speed, until the shells are broken into small pieces. Transfer the mixture to a large saucepan, and add 6 cups water along with the wine, bay leaves, peppercorns, and reserved liquid. Bring to a simmer over medium-low heat and cook, stirring occasionally, for about 45 minutes.

Strain the stock through a fine-mesh strainer into a bowl, pressing down on the solids with the back of a spoon to extract as much liquid as possible. Discard the solids. (You can make the stock ahead of time and refrigerate or freeze.)

Heat the oil in a medium saucepan over medium heat until it is smoking, about 3 minutes. Gradually add the flour, whisking constantly, and then cook until the roux is the color of mahogany (one shade darker than peanut butter), about 2 minutes. Quickly transfer the roux to a metal bowl to stop the cooking.

Melt 2 tablespoons of the butter in another medium saucepan over medium-high heat. Add the tomatoes, shallots, leek, celery, bell pepper, and Creole seasoning and cook, stirring occasionally, for 10 minutes. Deglaze the pan with the ⅓ cup Armagnac and cook, stirring, for 2 minutes. Add the lobster stock, whisking constantly. Bring the bisque to a simmer and whisk in the roux. Reduce the heat to medium-low and simmer, skimming any foam that may rise to the surface for 60 minutes. Stir in the remaining 2 tablespoons butter and the cream, splash of Armagnac, and thyme. Adjust the seasoning with salt and pepper if necessary.

Puree the bisque, in batches, in a blender and then pour it through a fine-mesh strainer set over a saucepan. (The bisque can be made up to this point 2 days ahead; cover and refrigerate.) Heat the bisque over medium-low heat until hot, then add the reserved lobster meat and serve.

HOMEY ROUX

At Commander's Palace, we make all our roux in large volumes on the stove. When cooking at home, you can use the microwave; it's quick and foolproof. Here's how to do it: In a 4-cup glass measuring cup, stir together ½ cup flour and ½ cup vegetable oil. Microwave, covered, on high power for 2 minutes. Stir, and microwave for another 2 minutes. Stir, and continue these 2-minute intervals until a deep, dark mahogany color is achieved.

Cognac Shrimp with Andouille Cracked-Corn Grits

Shrimp and grits are low-country fare, but we've given them a whole new attitude here. The mushrooms, demi-glace, cognac, and healthy amount of Creole seasoning help with the transformation.

• SERVES 4 AS A MAIN COURSE •

24 large shrimp (16 to 20 per pound), peeled and deveined

4 teaspoons Creole seasoning, store-bought or homemade (see box, page 9)

4 teaspoons vegetable oil

4 tablespoons (½ stick) unsalted butter, cut into pieces

1 tablespoon minced garlic

1 leek (white part only), halved lengthwise, sliced thin, and rinsed well

8 ounces assorted mushrooms, such as cremini, shiitake, chanterelle, and portobello, wiped clean and chopped (remove shiitake stems)

½ cup cognac or brandy

1 cup peeled, seeded, and chopped tomatoes

½ cup seafood stock or water

¼ cup veal demi-glace (available at gourmet markets)

½ teaspoon kosher salt

¼ teaspoon freshly ground black pepper

1 tablespoon chopped fresh thyme

Andouille Cracked-Corn Grits (page 189)

1 cup sliced green onions (green part only)

In a large bowl, toss the shrimp with 3 teaspoons of the Creole seasoning.

In a large skillet, heat 2 teaspoons of the oil over medium-high heat. Add half of the shrimp and sear until half cooked, about 40 seconds. Transfer the shrimp to a large plate, and repeat with the remaining 2 teaspoons oil and remaining shrimp.

Return the skillet to high heat. Add 2 tablespoons of the butter and the garlic and sauté, stirring and scraping the bottom of the skillet, until the garlic is fragrant, 30 seconds. Add the leek, reduce the heat to medium, and cook, stirring, until the leek is soft and golden brown, about 1½ minutes. Add the mushrooms and cook until they are soft and give off their liquid, about 2 minutes.

Remove the skillet from the heat and carefully add the cognac (watch out for flare-ups). Return the skillet to the heat and cook for about 1½ minutes. Then add the tomatoes, stock, demi-glace, salt, and pepper and bring to a simmer over medium heat. Cook until slightly reduced, about 2 minutes. Add the shrimp and thyme and cook, stirring, until the shrimp are warmed through, about 1 minute. Remove the skillet from the heat and stir in the remaining 2 tablespoons butter, several pieces at a time. Add the remaining 1 teaspoon Creole seasoning, and taste for seasoning.

Serve over Andouille Cracked-Corn Grits and garnish with the green onions.

CLEANING LEEKS

Leeks are grown in dirt and are full of the stuff by the time they get to your kitchen. The best way to clean them is to slice them first, then soak them in a big bowl of water. The dirt and sand will sink and the leeks will float, so they can be easily skimmed away.

CRAB AND BRIE–STUFFED FLOUNDER

This is a great recipe for holiday entertaining. The flavors of fresh crab, flounder, and Brie combine exquisitely, and the dish is truly impressive when it is drizzled with the Armagnac cream—which, happily for the cook, can be made ahead of time. This is one of the most requested dishes at the Chef's Table at Commander's Palace and always draws a crowd in the kitchen before it's presented to our guests.

• SERVES 4 AS A MAIN COURSE •

6 teaspoons vegetable oil

4 small flounder (about 1 pound each), filleted, keeping the tail intact (see box, page 174)

Kosher salt

Ground white pepper

4 ounces Brie cheese, at room temperature

4 tablespoons (½ stick) unsalted butter, at room temperature

¼ cup thinly sliced green onions (green part only, cut on the bias)

12 ounces jumbo lump crabmeat, picked over for shells and cartilage

ARMAGNAC CREAM SAUCE

2½ tablespoons unsalted butter

3 tablespoons minced shallots

¼ teaspoon kosher salt

¼ teaspoon ground white pepper

2 sprigs fresh thyme

4 tablespoons Armagnac or brandy

3 tablespoons dry white wine

1¼ cups heavy cream

SAUTÉED TOMATOES AND SPINACH

2 tablespoons unsalted butter

1 tablespoon minced garlic

1 pint small tomatoes, such as cherry or teardrop, halved

4 cups baby spinach

Salt and pepper to taste

½ teaspoon minced fresh tarragon

2 tablespoons minced fresh chives

Preheat the oven to 425°F. Lightly grease a large baking sheet with 2 teaspoons of the vegetable oil.

Season the inside pocket of each fish fillet with a pinch each of salt and white pepper.

With the back of a wooden spoon, combine the Brie, butter, green onions, 1 tablespoon salt, and ½ teaspoon white pepper in a bowl, mixing until well combined. Gently fold in the crabmeat, being careful not to break up the lumps.

Open the fish and arrange the stuffing down the center, spreading it along the length of the fillet. Fold the fillets over to enclose the stuffing, and transfer them to the prepared baking sheet. Rub 1 teaspoon of the remaining oil over the top of each fish, and season with a pinch of kosher salt. Cook for 16 to 20 minutes, until the fish are cooked through, firm and springy, and the stuffing is hot.

Meanwhile, prepare the Armagnac cream sauce: Melt 2 tablespoons of the butter in a medium skillet over medium-high heat. Add the shallots, salt, and white pepper and cook, stirring, until the shallots are translucent, about 2 minutes. Add the thyme sprigs and stir. Add 3 tablespoons of the Armagnac and the white wine, return to a simmer, and reduce until nearly all the liquid has evaporated, 2 to 3 minutes. Add the cream and cook until reduced by half, 4 to 5 minutes. Add the remaining 1 tablespoon Armagnac and remove from the heat. Strain the sauce through a fine-mesh strainer into a small, clean saucepan and keep it warm. (The sauce can be made up to 1 day ahead; cover, and refrigerate. Reheat gently before serving.)

Prepare the sautéed tomatoes and spinach: Place a medium skillet over medium-high heat and heat it for 3 minutes. Add the remaining 2 tablespoons butter and swirl to coat the bottom. Add the garlic and cook, stirring, for 15 seconds. Add the tomatoes, spinach, and a pinch of salt and pepper, then toss until the spinach is lightly wilted, 1 minute. Add the tarragon, and pour off any excess liquid.

Divide the spinach mixture among four plates, top with the fish, and drizzle with the sauce. Garnish with the chives.

POCKET CUT

Ask your fishmonger to give you a pocket cut on the flounder, which means all bones (spine and pin bones) are removed, leaving the tail intact to hold the two fish fillets together.

TORY IMPROV

If you like the idea of stuffed fish but are in a hurry, omit the Armagnac cream and the sautéed tomatoes and spinach. You'll still end up with a fantastic, elegant dinner.

No flounder? Any type of soft, white, flaky fish can be used here (whole or just fillets), such as speckled trout, drum, sheepshead, or rainbow trout.

SPECKLED TROUT NAPOLEONS WITH MOREL CREAM

This dish highlights mushrooms, so all you mushroom lovers out there, this is for you. You could save the napoleons for a fancy dinner party, but better yet, do it just for you. Phyllo dough is one of those ingredients chefs use often but most home cooks don't take enough advantage of. It is simple to work with and makes for beautifully presented dishes.

• SERVES 4 AS A MAIN COURSE •

PHYLLO SQUARES

3 sheets phyllo dough, thawed if frozen

2 tablespoons unsalted butter, melted

MOREL CREAM

½ ounce dried morel mushrooms

2 cups heavy cream

¼ cup dry white wine

⅛ teaspoon kosher salt

⅛ teaspoon ground white pepper

2¼ cups dry white wine

2 cups seafood stock or water

4 fresh parsley stems

5 whole black peppercorns

2 bay leaves

Kosher salt

Eight 3- to 3½-ounce speckled trout fillets

6 tablespoons (¾ stick) unsalted butter

4 ounces assorted wild mushrooms, such as chanterelle, morel, shiitake, oyster, and/or cremini, wiped clean and stems trimmed (remove shiitake stems)

1⅛ teaspoons freshly ground black pepper

1 pound jumbo lump or lump crabmeat, picked over for shells and cartilage

½ cup thinly sliced green onions (green part only)

Pinch of ground white pepper

Four 4-inch fresh rosemary stems, bottom 2 inches of leaves pulled off

Prepare the phyllo squares: Preheat the oven to 300°F. Lightly butter a baking sheet.

Lay 1 sheet of phyllo on a work surface with the long side facing you, and lightly brush the top with some of the melted butter. Top with a second sheet of phyllo and brush it with butter. Lay the third sheet on the stack and brush it with the remaining butter. With a thin, sharp knife, cut the phyllo in half lengthwise, and then in half vertically, making four rectangles. Cut each rectangle in half to make eight rectangles total. Lay the rectangles on the prepared baking sheet and top with another baking sheet to help them remain flat. Bake for about 15 minutes, until the phyllo stacks are dry and barely golden brown. Remove the top baking sheet and let the phyllo cool on the bottom baking sheet. (The phyllo stacks can be made 1 day ahead and kept in an airtight container at room temperature.)

Prepare the morel cream: Grind the mushrooms to a fine dust in a spice grinder. Combine the cream, wine, salt, and pepper in a medium saucepan, bring to a simmer, and cook until the cream is reduced by half, 10 to 11 minutes. Keep warm. Reserve the mushroom dust in a small ramekin.

In a large, deep skillet or a roasting pan set over two burners, combine 2 cups of the wine with the stock, parsley stems, peppercorns, bay leaves, and 1 teaspoon salt. Bring to a boil. Then reduce the heat to medium-low and simmer for 5 minutes. Season the fish on all sides with salt and pepper, then add the fish to the simmering liquid and poach until just cooked through, 7 to 9 minutes.

Meanwhile, heat a small skillet over medium-high heat for 2 minutes. Add 2 tablespoons of the butter. When it has melted, add the mushrooms, ⅛ teaspoon salt, and the black pepper and cook, stirring, until the mushrooms are soft and have given off their liquid, 3 to 4 minutes.

Melt the remaining 4 tablespoons butter in a medium skillet over medium heat. Add the crabmeat, remaining ¼ cup wine, green onions, and a pinch each of salt and white pepper, and cook, stirring slightly, being careful not to break up the lumps, until warmed through, about 2 minutes.

Spoon the morel cream onto four large plates. Arrange each trout fillet on top of the cream and top it with an eighth of the mushrooms and the crab. Crown with a phyllo crisp, then repeat with more fish, mushrooms, crab, and so on. Skewer a rosemary sprig through the phyllo crisp to keep the stack from tipping over.

Creole Cream Cheese Gnocchi with Crawfish

Creole cream cheese combined with gnocchi, crawfish, and chanterelle mushrooms is about as decadent as it gets. We make our own Creole cream cheese, which is quite different than regular cream cheese—it's tart and has a smoother, more liquefied texture. If you order some (see Resources), you won't regret it. (Another favorite way of eating Creole cream cheese is with sugar and berries.) If you can't get Creole cream cheese, substitute sour cream or crème fraîche.

When making gnocchi, you need to work fast because if the potato in the dough gets cold, it gets too starchy and sticky to work with and won't bind with the other ingredients. It becomes potato glue.

• SERVES 4 AS A FIRST COURSE •

Gnocchi

One 1-pound russet potato

1¼ cups all-purpose flour, plus additional for dusting

4 tablespoons (½ stick) unsalted butter, melted

2 tablespoons Creole cream cheese

½ teaspoon kosher salt

½ teaspoon ground white pepper

2 large egg yolks

1 tablespoon vegetable oil

Crawfish Sauce

1 tablespoon unsalted butter

2 tablespoons minced shallots

8 ounces cooked Louisiana crawfish tails

2 ounces tasso, minced (see box, page 10)

2 ounces chanterelle mushrooms, wiped clean and torn into pieces

¼ teaspoon Creole seasoning, store-bought or homemade (see box, page 9)

¾ cup heavy cream

2 tablespoons Creole cream cheese

1 teaspoon truffle oil

½ teaspoon chopped fresh tarragon

Salt and white pepper

Prepare the gnocchi: Place the potato in a medium saucepan and add cold water to cover; salt the water. Bring the water to a boil over medium heat and cook until the potato is tender, about 30 minutes. Drain. Holding the hot potato in a kitchen towel–covered hand, peel off the skin (only) with a knife. Run the potato through a ricer or a food mill.

Combine the potato with the flour, melted butter, Creole cream cheese, salt, and white pepper in a large bowl, and stir with a rubber spatula until the mixture is smooth and the flour is completely incorporated, about 15 seconds. Add the egg yolks and stir for 15 seconds more, being careful not to overwork the dough. Turn the dough out onto a floured work surface, and cut it into eight portions.

Working with one portion at a time, roll your hands back and forth over the dough, outward from the center to the ends, to form a long, thin strand, about ½ inch in diameter. Cut each dough strand into ½-inch pieces and sprinkle the tops lightly with flour. (Add as little flour as possible to prevent sticking.) Using the edge of a large knife or bench scraper, lift the gnocchi from the work surface and transfer them to a baking sheet.

Bring a large pot of salted water to a boil. Fill a large bowl with ice and water, and set it aside.

Stir all of the gnocchi into the boiling water and cook, undisturbed, until they start to float, 3 to 3½ minutes. Remove them with a slotted spoon or strainer, and place them in the ice water to stop the cooking. Drain the gnocchi, transfer them to a large bowl, and toss with the oil. (The gnocchi can be made up to 1 day ahead, covered, and refrigerated; or they can be frozen. If you are making them ahead, toss the gnocchi with extra vegetable oil to prevent sticking.)

Prepare the crawfish sauce: Heat a large skillet over medium-high heat for about 1 minute. Add the butter and shallots, and cook until the shallots are wilted, about 30 seconds. Add the crawfish, tasso, mushrooms, and Creole seasoning and cook, stirring, for 2 minutes. Add the heavy cream and bring to a simmer. Add the gnocchi and cook until they are hot and the sauce is slightly thickened, 2 minutes. Stir in the Creole cream cheese, truffle oil, and tarragon, and cook for 30 seconds. Adjust the seasoning as necessary.

THE POTATO BEHIND THE CHEF

Potatoes made Tory become a chef. When he was a child, while his mom and grandmother were making dinner they would occupy him by giving him a warm baked potato to play with. He sat at the kitchen table, completely fascinated with kneading the potato in his hands and transforming it from a fluffy, crumbly potato into play dough. Everyone tells their children not to play with their food, but Tory's mom let him, and it sparked his food curiosity.

Seared Scallops with Foie Gras and Citrus Beurre Blanc

We love sea scallops. They're soft, succulent, moist, and naturally sweet. And they have never been so indulgent as they are here, paired with foie gras and a citrus-spiked butter sauce. Unfortunately most restaurants overcook scallops or, God forbid, deep-fry them. We like our scallops medium-rare and seared to a golden brown on the outside. Buy scallops that are a bit sticky to the touch, smell sweet, and look dry; they should never be sitting in a white milky solution.

• SERVES 4 AS A FIRST COURSE •

Citrus Beurre Blanc

1 cup dry white wine

1 cup fresh orange juice

1 medium lemon, peel and pith removed, sliced crosswise

1 medium shallot, sliced thin

10 whole black peppercorns

1 bay leaf

3 tablespoons heavy cream

4 tablespoons (½ stick) cold unsalted butter, cut into pieces

1½ teaspoons sugar

¼ teaspoon ground white pepper

⅛ teaspoon kosher salt

8 large dry-pack sea scallops (about 12 ounces total)

1¼ teaspoons kosher salt

½ teaspoon ground white pepper

2 teaspoons vegetable oil

8 ounces cold foie gras, sliced into four ½-inch-thick pieces

¾ teaspoon freshly ground black pepper

Prepare the citrus beurre blanc: Combine the wine, orange juice, lemon slices, shallot, peppercorns, and bay leaf in a medium saucepan and bring to a boil over medium-high heat. Reduce the heat to medium and simmer until thickened and reduced to about ½ cup, 15 minutes. Add the cream, return to a simmer, and cook until reduced again to ½ cup, 1 to 2 minutes. Remove the saucepan from the heat and add the butter, several pieces at a time, whisking constantly until the sauce is thick and emulsified. Strain the sauce through a fine-mesh strainer into a small saucepan, and stir in the sugar, white pepper, and salt. Keep warm.

Arrange the scallops on a paper towel–lined plate, top with another layer of paper towels, and chill for 10 minutes to wick away any moisture.

Season both sides of the scallops with ½ teaspoon of the salt and the white pepper. Heat the oil in a large skillet over high heat until it is hot but not smoking. Add the scallops, leaving space between them, and cook undisturbed until seared and golden brown, 2 minutes on each side. Transfer the scallops to a platter and keep warm.

Carefully wipe the skillet clean with paper towels, and return it to high heat. Cut a light crosshatch pattern into the top of the foie gras and season with the remaining ¾ teaspoon salt and the black pepper. Cook the foie gras, in two batches, for 15 seconds on each side.

Pool the citrus beurre blanc on four plates. Arrange 2 scallops in each pool, and top the scallops with a slice of foie gras.

BEURRE BLANC BASICS

This classic French butter sauce is a little finicky, but worth all the attention. If it gets too hot or cold, it will break. To avoid this, add your butter in small amounts and do it off the heat. Ideally, you want the sauce at about body temperature while adding the butter, so move your saucepan on and off the heat to regulate the temperature.

CRAB AND OYSTER
MUSHROOM RISOTTO

This is a truly memorable risotto. Crabmeat and oyster mushrooms speak of luxury, and here crabmeat chunks glisten on top of the rice like jewels.

• MAKES 3 CUPS; SERVES 4 AS A FIRST COURSE •

¼ cup cold heavy cream

Pinch of kosher salt

Pinch of ground white pepper

3½ cups seafood stock or water

4 tablespoons (½ stick) unsalted butter

1 shallot, minced

1 cup arborio or canaroli rice

3 ounces oyster mushrooms, stems removed, wiped clean and sliced

1 cup dry white wine

CRABMEAT TOPPING

4 tablespoons (½ stick) unsalted butter

2 tablespoons dry white wine

Pinch of kosher salt

Pinch of ground white pepper

8 ounces jumbo lump crabmeat, picked over for shells and cartilage

1 tablespoon minced fresh chives

1½ teaspoons minced fresh oregano, optional

1 teaspoon truffle oil, optional

Combine the cream, salt, and white pepper in a medium bowl and whisk until thick and doubled in volume. Cover and refrigerate until ready to use.

Bring the stock to a simmer in a medium saucepan. Reduce the heat to low, cover, and keep warm.

Melt the butter in medium skillet over medium-high heat. Add the shallot and cook, stirring, until soft, 1 minute. Add the rice and cook, stirring constantly with a wooden spoon, for 2 minutes. Add the mushrooms and cook, stirring, 30 seconds. Add the wine and cook until the liquid has nearly all evaporated, 2 minutes.

Add ¼ cup of the hot stock and cook, stirring constantly, until nearly all of it has evaporated, about 2 minutes. Cook the risotto, continuing to stir in the hot stock ¼ cup at a time and waiting until all the stock has evaporated before adding more, until the rice is almost soft and still slightly firm, or almost al dente, 20 to 30 minutes total. Turn down the heat and let the risotto stand while you prepare the crab.

Prepare the crabmeat topping: Combine the butter, wine, salt, and white pepper in a small skillet, and heat over medium heat until the butter has melted. Add the crabmeat and cook, being careful not to break up the lumps, until it is warmed through, about 2 minutes. Remove from the heat and add the chives.

Turn up the heat under the risotto and finish cooking. Then gently fold in the whipped cream, and the oregano if using, with a rubber spatula. Serve the risotto topped with the crabmeat and drizzle with the truffle oil if desired.

TORY'S RISOTTO TECHNIQUE

The smooth, velvety texture of risotto depends upon proper cooking technique. The first step is to make risotto in a wide saucepan or a skillet, so that the heat gets evenly distributed throughout the rice. Also be sure to wait and make sure all the hot liquid has been absorbed by the rice before adding more; you should be able to see the bottom of the pan between the liquid additions. Stir the risotto constantly and hang out by the stove, because there's only about a 4-minute window between perfectly cooked rice and mush. We always finish the risotto with whipped cream for lightness—it helps maintain the velvety texture during the time it takes to get the risotto out of the pan and to the table.

Pepper-Crusted Beef Sirloin with Crispy Oysters and Horseradish Cream

Beef and oysters are New Orleans' version of surf-and-turf. We amplify the flavor by crusting the steak with coarsely ground pepper, just like a steak au poivre. Top sirloin steak is cheaper than filet and prime rib, but it packs a wallop of beefiness.

• SERVES 4 •

Horseradish Cream

1½ cups heavy cream

2 tablespoons white vinegar

¼ cup prepared horseradish

Pinch of kosher salt

Pinch of freshly ground black
   pepper

1 cup all-purpose flour

1 cup masa flour (masa harina)

¼ cup Creole seasoning, store-bought
   or homemade (see box, page 9), plus
   additional to taste

Vegetable oil for frying, plus
   2 tablespoons

2 tablespoons kosher salt

Four 12-ounce beef top sirloin steaks

¼ cup coarsely ground black pepper

12 shucked oysters

¼ cup chopped fresh parsley

Prepare the horseradish cream: Combine the cream and vinegar in a small saucepan and cook over medium heat until reduced by half, about 5 minutes. Add the horseradish, salt, and pepper, and cook for 3 minutes. Keep warm.

Combine the all-purpose flour, masa flour, and ¼ cup Creole seasoning in a bowl. Set aside.

Heat 3 inches of oil in a large pot to 350°F. Meanwhile, heat a large cast-iron skillet over high heat until it is very hot, 3 minutes.

Sprinkle the salt on both sides of the steaks and rub it in. Sprinkle the pepper over the steaks and press with your fingers to form a crust. Pour the 2 tablespoons oil into the hot skillet and swirl it around. Arrange the steaks in the skillet, leaving ample space between them, and cook for 4 to 5 minutes on each side for medium-rare. Transfer the steaks to a platter and let rest while you fry the oysters.

Dredge the oysters in the seasoned flour, tossing them with your fingers to coat them until they are very dry. Fry the oysters in the hot oil, in two batches, until golden brown, about 1½ minutes. Transfer the oysters to paper towels to drain, and season them with additional Creole seasoning.

Serve the steaks in pools of the horseradish sauce, topped with the oysters and garnished with the parsley.

BEST-TASTING STEAKS

Tory always removes steaks from the refrigerator ahead of time in order to take the chill off them. This allows the temperature of the steak to rise a little and ensures more even cooking and a consistent pink color throughout. Also, always salt steaks first, then season with pepper. The salt quickly dissolves, leaving room for the pepper to stick.

SENSATIONAL SIDES

I T SEEMS TO US THAT MOST PEOPLE order main dishes because of the sides that accompany them. At least that's what we do when we go out to eat. Also, we believe that some dishes are just made for each other, like shrimp and grits. That being the case, we've dreamed up more creative, enticing sides at Commander's than we can remember, and here's a sampling. Some feature pretty humble, inexpensive, everyday ingredients like potatoes—but boy, are those potatoes good when they get gussied up with a bit of Creole mustard, sour cream, and green onions! Our choices will fit with what you're fixing and will pump up the flavor of everything on the plate.

SENSATIONAL SIDES

ROASTED BEET SALAD

Any volume of beets can be cooked in this manner—simply increase the amount of oil and seasoning proportionately. We call for both yellow and red beets for their contrasting colors, but you can use just red beets. This salad is especially good while still warm.

• SERVES 6 •

1½ pounds mixed red and yellow beets, trimmed and rinsed clean

½ teaspoon vegetable oil

Kosher salt and freshly ground black pepper to taste

6 tablespoons olive oil

2 tablespoons cane vinegar

2 tablespoons finely chopped fresh chives

1 tablespoon truffle oil

Preheat the oven to 400°F.

Place the beets in a baking dish, rub them with the vegetable oil, and season lightly with salt and pepper. Wrap the dish tightly with aluminum foil and roast for about 1 hour, until tender. Test doneness by inserting a toothpick into the center of each beet. They should be soft and the toothpick should pass through with little resistance.

Unwrap the beets and let them sit until they are cool enough to handle. Then rub the beets firmly with paper towels to remove the skin. Cut the ends off the beets and slice them ¼ inch thick. Place the beet slices in a bowl and toss with the remaining ingredients. Season with salt and pepper to taste.

ANDOUILLE CRACKED-CORN GRITS

Like everything in life, there are grits and then there are grits. Make the effort to get stone-ground grits and you will understand why some people compare grits to polenta: creamy, rich, and oh-so-flavorful. We buy ours from Anson Mills, where they freeze the corn and then grind it with freezing-cold equipment, preserving the intense corn flavor (see Resources). Grits are truly versatile—as comfortable with eggs at breakfast as with Cognac Shrimp (page 171), roasted meat, and fish.

• MAKES 3 CUPS; SERVES 4 •

6 tablespoons (¾ stick) unsalted butter

4 ounces andouille sausage, chopped

½ onion, diced

1 tablespoon Creole seasoning,
    store-bought or homemade
    (see box, page 9)

4 cups milk

1½ teaspoons kosher salt

1 teaspoon freshly ground black pepper

1 cup coarsely ground stone-ground
    yellow grits, rinsed

Melt the butter in a medium saucepan over medium heat. Add the andouille, onion, and Creole seasoning and cook, stirring occasionally, until the sausage starts to shrink, about 4 minutes. Add the milk, salt, and pepper, increase the heat, and bring to a boil. Slowly whisk in the grits, a few tablespoons at a time. Once all the grits are completely incorporated, bring to a simmer. Reduce the heat to medium-low and cook, stirring often with a wooden spoon, until the grits are tender, about 1 hour (depending on the grind of the grits).

Andouille Spoonbread

This spoonbread has a little more flair than classic versions. It is a perfect vehicle for soaking up all the juices from the Apple and Bourbon–Braised Pheasant (page 83).

• SERVES 6 •

3 tablespoons unsalted butter, plus
    additional for greasing ramekins

1½ cups fresh corn kernels (about
    2 ears)

1½ cups milk

¾ cup (about 3 ounces) diced andouille
    sausage

1½ teaspoons Creole seasoning,
    store-bought or homemade
    (see box, page 9)

1 cup yellow cornmeal

4 large eggs, separated

½ teaspoon baking powder

Preheat the oven to 325°F. Grease six 6-ounce ramekins or one 8-inch round soufflé dish.

In a medium saucepan, combine the corn kernels, milk, andouille, butter, and Creole seasoning, and bring to a boil over medium heat. Whisk in the cornmeal and cook for 5 minutes, until the mixture is mushy and the cornmeal doesn't taste so gritty. Remove from the heat.

In a large bowl, whisk together the egg yolks and baking powder for 1 minute. Stir in the cornmeal mixture.

In a large bowl or a standing mixer, beat the egg whites on high speed until stiff peaks form. Using a rubber spatula, fold the egg whites into the cornmeal mixture. Transfer the mixture to the prepared ramekins, place them on a baking sheet, and bake for 15 minutes, until golden brown and puffed and a toothpick inserted in the center comes out clean. (If using a single soufflé dish, bake for 25 minutes, until cooked through.)

SHRIMP AND MIRLITON CASSEROLE

When Tory first moved to New Orleans in the spring of 1993, he thought he knew what good food was. Soon enough, he realized he didn't have a clue. Eman Loubier, his first supervisor in the Commander's kitchen, had him prepare this dish. When Tory first saw the recipe, he gathered the ingredients, head hung low and disappointed that one of his first tasks was to make "casserole," a dish he remembers his mom making with canned tuna, peas, and cream of mushroom soup. Upon reading through the recipe several more times and talking to the other people in the garde manger, he realized that this was a great staple of Creole cooking. Creole cooking is really all about taking the finest local ingredients, as lowly as they may seem, and combining them with the right techniques and the right seasoning.

Mirlitons, also called chayotes, grow all over Louisiana, and are practically flavorless on their own. The mirlitons in this homey, old-fashioned casserole get a new lease on life with tasso, garlic, fresh herbs, and Creole seasoning.

We make our own tasso, andouille, and other sausages in the upstairs butcher shop at Commander's Palace. If you can't find tasso, use a heavily smoked ham and increase the Creole seasoning.

· SERVES 10 AS A SIDE DISH ·

6 mirlitons (about 5 pounds total)
8 tablespoons (1 stick) unsalted butter
1 pound tasso, diced (see box, page 10)
1½ cups finely chopped onions
2 tablespoons minced garlic
1 pound small shrimp, peeled and deveined
1 tablespoon chopped fresh thyme

1 teaspoon Creole seasoning, store-bought or homemade (see box, page 9), or to taste
Kosher salt and freshly ground black pepper to taste
½ cup shrimp stock or canned low-sodium chicken broth
1½ cups fine dry bread crumbs

Preheat the oven to 350°F. Butter a 9×13-inch baking dish.

Peel the mirlitons with a vegetable peeler, halve them lengthwise, and then chop the flesh around the large seed.

Bring a medium saucepan of salted water to a boil. Add the mirlitons and cook over high heat until soft, about 7 minutes. Drain.

Melt the butter in a large skillet over medium-high heat. Add the tasso and cook, stirring, until it begins to shrink, about 4 minutes. Add the onions and garlic and sauté, stirring, until the onions are translucent, about 4 minutes. Add the mirlitons, shrimp, and thyme and cook, stirring, until the shrimp turn pink, about 2 minutes. Add the Creole seasoning and adjust the seasoning with salt and pepper. Add the stock and bring to a boil. Add the bread crumbs and cook, stirring, for 1 minute. Spoon the mixture into the prepared baking dish and bake for 25 minutes, until golden brown.

BACON-SMOTHERED GREEN BEANS

A great neighbor to the Coffee-Lacquered Stuffed Quail (page 92).

• SERVES 4 •

6 tablespoons chopped bacon

1 tablespoon unsalted butter

1 cup thinly sliced red onions

⅛ teaspoon salt

⅛ teaspoon freshly ground black pepper

3 cups cut-up green beans (ends trimmed, cut in half on the bias)

1 cup chicken stock or canned low-sodium chicken broth

Heat a medium skillet over medium heat for 1 minute. Add the bacon and butter and cook, stirring, for 1 minute. Add the onions, salt, and pepper and cook, stirring, for 1 minute. Add the green beans and stock and bring to a boil. Reduce the heat and simmer, uncovered, until the beans are tender and the liquid has evaporated, about 10 minutes.

Cajun Potato Salad

Most potato salads we've encountered are dull. Not this version—it is seasoned assertively and is a delicious side for po'boys and grilled game.

• MAKES 2 CUPS; SERVES 4 •

1 pound red potatoes, unpeeled

1 teaspoon Creole seasoning, store-bought or homemade (see box, page 9), plus additional for potato cooking water

½ teaspoon Tabasco sauce, plus additional for potato cooking water

½ cup mayonnaise

2 tablespoons minced celery

2 tablespoons Creole mustard

1 tablespoon minced jalapeño pepper

2 teaspoons minced shallots

Place the potatoes in a large pot and add water to cover. Season the water with Creole seasoning and Tabasco to taste (the water should taste spicy). Bring to a boil. Then reduce the heat and cook until tender, 30 minutes. Drain.

In a large bowl, combine the mayonnaise, celery, mustard, jalapeño, shallots, 1 teaspoon Creole seasoning, and ½ teaspoon Tabasco. Add the warm potatoes, pressing with the back of a spoon to smash them slightly.

TORY'S TIP

Don't overmix this potato salad or it will become sticky like glue. Also, remember that potatoes absorb more dressing when they're warm. This potato salad is best eaten the same day it's prepared, and may require more mayonnaise depending on the temperature at which you eat it.

TRUFFLED CELERY ROOT MASH

Celery root, also called celeriac, is an underused vegetable in the United States. It has a wonderfully fragrant, celery-tasting bulb underneath the knobby brown skin. This is perfect with Morel-Dusted Sheepshead with Pinot Noir Reduction (page 28).

• SERVES 4 •

2 large celery roots, peeled and coarsely chopped (6 cups)

5 cups milk

2 tablespoons unsalted butter

1 tablespoon white truffle oil

1 teaspoon kosher salt, plus additional to taste

½ teaspoon freshly ground black pepper, plus additional to taste

Combine the celery root and milk in a medium saucepan and bring to a simmer. Cook until tender, 15 to 20 minutes.

Drain the celery root into a colander set over a bowl; reserve the cooking liquid. Place the celery root, butter, truffle oil, salt, and pepper in a food processor and process until smooth, gradually adding ½ cup of the cooking liquid through the feed tube to ensure a smooth consistency. Adjust the seasoning to taste.

COCONUT CURRY RICE

This spicy, creamy rice makes a good match with a range of Caribbean-influenced dishes, from Jamaican Jerk Mahimahi (page 38) to Tory's Favorite Fish Tacos (page 40).

• SERVES 4 •

1 cup long-grain white rice

2 tablespoons vegetable oil

1 onion, chopped fine

2 teaspoons curry powder

2 teaspoons sugar

1 teaspoon kosher salt

1 teaspoon ground white pepper

1 bay leaf

1 cup unsweetened coconut
   milk

Place the rice in a medium bowl and rinse well under cold running water, running your fingers through the rice to remove the starch, until the water runs clear, about 2 minutes. Drain the rice well in a fine-mesh strainer.

Heat the oil in a large heavy saucepan over medium heat. Add the onion, curry powder, sugar, salt, white pepper, and bay leaf and cook, stirring, until the onion is translucent, 2½ to 3 minutes. Add the rice and stir for 30 seconds to coat it. Add 1¼ cups water and the coconut milk, and bring to a simmer. Reduce the heat to low, cover, and cook undisturbed until the rice has absorbed all the liquid and is no longer firm, 18 to 20 minutes. Remove and discard the bay leaf. Fluff the rice with a fork.

TOSTONES (FRIED PLANTAINS)

Plantains, like bananas, get darker as they ripen; for this recipe, the riper the plantain, the better and sweeter. When at the grocery store, look for yellow plantains with black spots. Plantains start out very green and move to yellow, then black. From green to black may take two weeks or more. These crisp, sweet, lush fried plantains are a delight alongside spicy food such as Jamaican Jerk Mahimahi (page 38) or smoked barbecued pork.

• MAKES ABOUT 12 SLICES; SERVES 4 •

One 14- to 16-ounce ripe plantain

Vegetable oil for frying

¼ teaspoon Creole seasoning, store-bought or homemade
(see box, page 9)

Cut the ends from the plantain and carefully run the tip of your knife along both sides to cut through the skin but not into the flesh. Place the plantain in a large bowl of hot water and let it sit for 5 minutes to loosen the skin.

Peel the skin from the plantain and cut the plantain on the bias into ½-inch-thick slices.

Fill a medium-size heavy pot halfway with oil and heat it to 350°F.

Fry the plantain slices until golden brown on all sides and just soft, 2½ to 3 minutes. Using a slotted spoon, transfer the plantains to paper towels to drain. While the plantains are still hot, press the slices firmly between two small plates to flatten them.

Return the oil to 350°F and refry the flattened plantain slices in a tostone press until deep golden brown and crisp, about 6 minutes. Drain them on paper towels again, and sprinkle with the Creole seasoning.

TORY'S TIP

Plantains are notoriously difficult to peel, but soaking them in hot water for about 5 minutes will loosen the skin right up. As with all fried food, season these plantains the second they come out of the oil so the seasoning sticks.

CREOLE SMASHED NEW POTATOES WITH SOUR CREAM, CREOLE MUSTARD, AND GREEN ONIONS

A bold version of mashed potatoes, these are great with the Braised Beef Short Ribs with Sweet Onions (page 133).

• MAKES 2 CUPS; SERVES 4 •

1 pound red potatoes, unpeeled, quartered

1 tablespoon kosher salt

3 tablespoons sour cream

2 tablespoons Creole mustard

2 tablespoons unsalted butter, at room temperature

1 tablespoon thinly sliced green onions (green part only)

2 teaspoons salt

1½ teaspoons black pepper

Place the potatoes in a small saucepan, cover with about 4 cups cold water, and add the salt. Bring the water to a boil and simmer until the potatoes are fork-tender, 15 minutes. Drain the potatoes and transfer them to a bowl. Add the sour cream, mustard, and butter, and smash with a wooden spoon until the mixture is slightly chunky. Stir in the green onions, and adjust the seasoning as desired.

FENNEL RAGOUT

This satisfying side is subtly flavored yet sophisticated and mates well with other delicate dishes, such as Crab and Brie–Stuffed Flounder (page 173) and Speckled Trout Napoleons with Morel Cream (page 175).

• MAKES 1½ CUPS; SERVES 4 •

4 tablespoons (½ stick) unsalted butter

2 large onions, sliced thin

2 fennel bulbs, sliced thin

¼ teaspoon kosher salt, plus additional to taste

¼ teaspoon ground white pepper, plus additional to taste

2 tablespoons Pernod, Herbsaint, or other anise-flavored liqueur

1 tablespoon sugar, plus additional to taste

Melt the butter in a large skillet over medium-low heat. Stir in the onions, fennel, salt, and white pepper, and reduce the heat to low. Cook, uncovered, stirring occasionally, until the vegetables are very soft, 20 to 25 minutes.

Remove the skillet from the heat and stir in the Pernod and sugar. Return the skillet to medium heat and cook, stirring, until the liquid has evaporated, about 1 minute. Adjust the seasoning with salt, white pepper, and sugar to taste.

TORY'S TIP

Fennel has a faint sweetness when raw, but it loses this as it cooks. Tory likes to add a bit of sugar to all of his fennel dishes at the end of cooking to bring the sweetness back.

WILD MUSHROOM AND ARTICHOKE CAKES

Who doesn't like wild mushrooms and artichokes? These cakes are wonderful with beef or game, or just about anything and everything. You can use canned artichokes in water, or frozen artichokes, in place of fresh artichokes. (Besides hearts of palm, artichoke is the only vegetable we almost like better canned than fresh.)

Do not stir the bread into the cooked vegetable mixture; this breaks up the bread and turns it into a mushy paste. Instead, gently fold in the bread and let it sit for 5 minutes to absorb the liquid.

• SERVES 8 •

6 tablespoons (¾ stick) unsalted butter

1 small leek (white part only), halved lengthwise, sliced thin, and rinsed well

1 tablespoon minced garlic

8 ounces assorted wild mushrooms (3 cups), sliced thin, such as chanterelle, morel, shiitake, oyster, and/or cremini, wiped clean and stems trimmed (remove shiitake stems)

2 whole cooked artichokes, hearts sliced thin (about 2 cups)

½ teaspoon kosher salt, plus additional to taste

½ teaspoon freshly ground black pepper, plus additional to taste

¼ cup brandy, optional

½ cup chicken stock or canned low-sodium chicken broth

3 cups cubed day-old French bread (¾-inch cubes)

1½ teaspoons minced fresh rosemary

1½ teaspoons minced fresh thyme

Melt 2 tablespoons of the butter in a large skillet over medium-high heat. Add the leek and garlic and cook, stirring, for about 2 minutes. Add the mushrooms, artichokes, salt, and pepper, and cook, stirring constantly, until the vegetables have given off their liquid and are soft, about 8 minutes. Add the brandy if using, and cook until evaporated, 30 to 45 seconds. Add the stock and cook until the liquid is reduced by half, 3 minutes.

Remove the skillet from the heat and fold in the bread cubes and the herbs. Let the mixture sit for 5 minutes for the bread to absorb the liquid. Adjust the seasoning with salt and pepper as needed. The mixture should be moist but pliable, damp but not wet. If it's too wet, add more bread; if it's too dry, add more stock.

Using your hands, form the mixture into 8 patties, and transfer them to a plate. Melt 2 tablespoons of the butter in a large skillet over medium heat. Add half of the cakes and cook until golden brown, 5 to 6 minutes on each side. Set them aside and keep warm. Melt the remaining 2 tablespoons butter in the skillet and cook the remaining cakes in the same manner.

BACON BRAISED CABBAGE

Fast, easy, and hugely flavorful, this cabbage dish will make you swoon. At Commander's Palace, we add pears for an element of complexity and fullness of flavor. By all means, if you have some at home, chop them and add them to the bacon.

• SERVES 4 •

2 cups chopped onions

1 cup chopped bacon

3 tablespoons unsalted butter

Pinch of kosher salt

Pinch of freshly ground black pepper

1 medium green cabbage, shredded (about 5 cups)

¼ cup cane vinegar

¼ cup dark brown sugar, packed

Heat a large Dutch oven over medium-high heat for 2 minutes. Add the onions, bacon, butter, salt, and pepper and cook, stirring, until the onions are caramelized, 4 to 5 minutes. Add the cabbage, vinegar, and brown sugar and cook, stirring occasionally, until the cabbage is wilted to half the original volume, about 5 minutes. Reduce the heat to medium-low and cook, uncovered, stirring frequently, until the cabbage is tender and all the moisture has evaporated, 30 minutes.

LEEK AND MUSHROOM BREAD PUDDING SOUFFLÉ

Savory bread puddings evolved from the classic New Orleans dessert. We serve them with roasts in place of dressings sometimes, but we fatten them up with cream.

• SERVES 10 •

2 cups heavy cream

6 large eggs

2½ teaspoons kosher salt

½ teaspoon freshly ground black pepper

1 large loaf French bread, sliced into ½-inch-thick rounds

4 tablespoons (½ stick) unsalted butter

¾ cup thinly sliced leeks (white part only), rinsed well

2 cups thinly sliced assorted wild mushrooms, such as chanterelle, morel, shiitake, oyster, and/or cremini, wiped clean and stems trimmed (remove shiitake stems)

1 tablespoon chopped fresh thyme

½ cup bourbon

In a large bowl, whisk together the cream, eggs, 2 teaspoons of the salt, and the pepper. Add the bread and let it soak for 1 hour to absorb the custard.

Preheat the oven to 250°F.

Melt the butter in a medium skillet over high heat. Add the leeks and sauté until soft, about 1½ minutes. Add the mushrooms and thyme and cook, stirring, for 4 minutes. Take the skillet off the heat, add the bourbon, and carefully ignite (watch out for flare-ups). Stir in the remaining ½ teaspoon salt.

Arrange half the bread in one layer in a 2-quart or 9 × 13-inch baking dish. Spoon the mushroom mixture over the bread. Arrange the remaining bread over the mushrooms and top with any remaining egg mixture, whisking as you pour to evenly distribute the pepper. Bake for 1 hour and 20 minutes, until an instant-read thermometer inserted in the center registers 140°F.

POTATO AND CARAMELIZED ONION GRATIN

Gratins are year-round crowd-pleasers, but this one is especially welcome in winter with a hearty stew such as the Black Bear Bourguignonne (page 122). You can make this ahead and reheat it just before serving.

• SERVES 4 •

1½ pounds russet potatoes

Kosher salt

¼ cup olive oil

1 small onion, halved lengthwise and very thinly sliced (julienned)

Pinch of freshly ground black pepper, plus additional to taste

1½ cups heavy cream

2 teaspoons finely chopped fresh thyme

2 teaspoons finely grated Parmigiano-Reggiano cheese

Slice the potatoes as thin as possible, using a knife or a manual slicer such as a mandoline. Place the potatoes in a large bowl, add ½ teaspoon salt, and mix thoroughly. Let rest for 30 minutes, tossing every 5 minutes. (This helps dry out the potatoes so that they won't oxidize too much as the onions cook.)

Heat the oil in a small skillet over medium heat. Add the onion, a pinch of salt, and the pepper and cook, stirring frequently, until the onion is caramelized and the skillet is dry, 10 minutes. Add the cream and bring to a boil. Remove from the heat and add the thyme.

Meanwhile, preheat the oven to 325°F. Grease an 8-inch square baking dish and set it aside.

Squeeze the potatoes by handfuls to expel as much liquid as possible. Transfer the potatoes to a large bowl and add the cream mixture, tossing to completely coat the potatoes. Adjust the seasoning to taste by taking a small piece of the potato—it's the only way to know if the seasoning is correct.

Spoon one quarter of the potato mixture into the prepared baking dish, using the back of a spoon to press the mixture firmly into the bottom and sides. Sprinkle the potatoes with ½ teaspoon of the cheese, and top with more potatoes.

Continue alternating for a total of four layers. Cover the dish tightly with plastic wrap and then with aluminum foil, and bake for 1½ hours, until the gratin is set and the liquid has been absorbed.

Carefully remove the aluminum foil and plastic wrap, and continue to cook the gratin in the oven uncovered for an additional 30 minutes to caramelize the surface. Let the gratin stand at room temperature for 20 to 30 minutes before serving.

THE SWEET FINISH

WE HATE DESSERTS THAT LOOK BETTER THAN THEY TASTE. Even great restaurants where the rest of the meal is perfect can get too cute when it comes to dessert, with flavors that fall flat and creations that don't live up to expectations. That's not what you'll find here. Years ago, Ti's mom, Ella Brennan, persuaded a chef to create a dessert that tasted like a brownie pulled out of the oven too soon. That's the kind of dessert we love, and the kind we feature here. Sticky gingerbread cupcakes, toffee bars, pound cake— real food that, unlike so many desserts, is worth every calorie. If you're going hunting or fishing, just make one of these desserts ahead of time and throw it in a self-seal bag. We just hope it makes it to dessert time and doesn't go missing on the car ride.

THE SWEET FINISH

STRAWBERRY TRIFLE WITH MINT JULEP PASTRY CREAM

On the way home from your fishing trip, stop in Ponchatoula, Louisiana, or wherever your best berries come from, and buy a few flats. These sweet biscuits soak up all the strawberry juices and get layered with rich, smooth pastry cream spiked with bourbon and mint.

Next time you make biscuits for breakfast, bake an extra batch and save them for this dessert. Or to cut down on prep time, use store-bought biscuits.

• SERVES 6 TO 8 •

SWEET BUTTERMILK BISCUITS

1¾ cups all-purpose flour, plus additional for working the dough

1¼ tablespoons sugar

1¼ teaspoons baking powder

¼ teaspoon salt

¼ teaspoon baking soda

8 tablespoons (1 stick) cold unsalted butter, cut into pieces

¾ cup cold buttermilk

6 cups strawberries, cleaned and quartered

1⅓ cups bourbon

2 tablespoons sugar

MINT JULEP PASTRY CREAM

5 tablespoons sugar

2½ tablespoons cornstarch

1 cup milk

4 large egg yolks

5 ounces cream cheese, cut into ½-inch cubes, at room temperature

3 tablespoons very thinly sliced fresh mint

2 tablespoons bourbon

½ teaspoon vanilla extract

Preheat the oven to 400°F.

Prepare the sweet buttermilk biscuits: Combine all the dry ingredients in a large bowl and whisk to combine. Add the butter, and using your fingers, work it into the dry ingredients until the mixture resembles small peas. Add the buttermilk and mix with your fingers just until the mixture comes together, being careful not to overwork it. Turn the dough out onto a lightly floured surface and pat it out to ¾-inch thickness. Cut biscuits out of the dough using a floured 2½-inch round cutter. Bake the biscuits on a greased baking sheet until golden brown, 18 to 20 minutes. Let them cool on a wire rack. (The biscuits can be made up to 3 days ahead and kept in an airtight container at room temperature.

In a large bowl, toss together the strawberries, bourbon, and sugar. Refrigerate, covered, for 1 hour and up to 4 hours.

Prepare the mint julep pastry cream: Whisk the sugar and cornstarch together in a medium-size heavy saucepan. Whisk in ¼ cup of the milk until smooth. In a medium bowl, whisk the remaining ¾ cup milk and the egg yolks; add this to the saucepan. Bring the mixture to a simmer and cook, stirring constantly with a rubber spatula, until the mixture is thick, 3 to 5 minutes. Remove the pan from the heat and add the cream cheese, a few cubes at a time, whisking after each addition until all the pieces are incorporated and the mixture is smooth. Whisk in the mint, bourbon, and vanilla. (The pastry cream can be made up to 2 days ahead; chill it with plastic wrap touching its surface.)

In a trifle dish or a large glass bowl, break half of the biscuits into large pieces. Top with a third of the berries and half of the pastry cream. Repeat the layers of biscuits, berries, and pastry cream. Top the trifle with the remaining berries. Chill until ready to serve.

Spicy Praline-Crusted Popcorn Balls

These balls are like a new improved Cracker Jack. They are spicy-sweet and addictive, and make a fabulous snack.

• MAKES 15 TO 18 BALLS •

1 cup (2 sticks) unsalted butter
1½ cups packed light brown sugar
½ cup light corn syrup

½ teaspoon Creole seasoning,
  store-bought or homemade
  (see box, page 9)
9 to 11 cups popped popcorn

Cover a large baking sheet with wax paper or parchment paper, and set it aside.

Place the butter, brown sugar, corn syrup, and Creole seasoning in a medium-size heavy saucepan and cook, stirring occasionally, over medium heat until the mixture reaches a dark caramel color and a candy thermometer registers 250°F, 10 to 12 minutes.

Place the popcorn in a very large bowl. Slowly drizzle the caramel over the popcorn and mix together with two heatproof spatulas. When the popcorn is cool enough to handle, form it into 3-inch balls and place them on the prepared baking sheet. Let the balls cool to room temperature, and serve.

MAGIC COOKIE BARS

This is the kind of irresistible bar you find in Junior League cookbooks all over the country, from the Pacific Northwest all the way down to the Southeast. We swank the bars up a bit with cashews, and sometimes macadamia nuts, and a mixture of dark and milk chocolate chips.

• MAKES 24 BARS •

1 cup cornflake or graham cracker crumbs

⅓ cup sugar

8 tablespoons (1 stick) unsalted butter

1 cup dark chocolate chips

1 cup milk chocolate chips

½ cup chopped walnuts

½ cup chopped salted cashews

1⅓ cups sweetened coconut flakes

One 14-ounce can sweetened condensed milk

Preheat the oven to 350°F.

Combine the crumbs and sugar in a medium bowl, and set aside.

Melt the butter in a small skillet over medium-high heat and cook, swirling the pan constantly, until the butter solids are a deep brown color, 4 to 5 minutes. Pour the butter over the crumb mixture and stir well to combine. Pour the mixture into a 9×13-inch baking dish and pack it evenly and tightly to form a crust, pressing the mixture down with the back of a spoon.

Layer half of both chocolate chips over the crust, top with half of the nuts, and then top that with half of the coconut. Repeat the layers of chocolate chips, nuts, and coconut. Slowly drizzle the condensed milk over the top to completely cover. Bake until golden brown and set, 28 to 30 minutes. Cool in the pan on a rack for 30 minutes. Then cut into 2-inch squares. (The bars can be kept in an airtight container at room temperature for up to 3 days, but we guarantee they won't last that long!)

CITRUS POUND CAKE WITH LEMON SHERBET AND CITRUS COMPOTE

This is exactly the kind of dessert you find in the homes of good cooks—not in restaurants. Invite us over. Really! We'll come.

• MAKES 1 LOAF CAKE; SERVES 8 •

CITRUS POUND CAKE

1 cup (2 sticks) plus 1 tablespoon unsalted butter, at room temperature

2 cups sugar

1½ tablespoons finely grated lemon zest

1½ tablespoons finely grated orange zest

5 medium eggs

2¼ cups cake flour

¼ teaspoon baking powder

½ teaspoon salt

½ cup buttermilk

¼ cup fresh lemon juice

CITRUS COMPOTE

1 medium grapefruit, peel and pith removed

1 medium lemon, peel and pith removed

1 medium lime, peel and pith removed

1 medium orange or satsuma, peel and pith removed

⅓ cup Grand Marnier

⅓ cup granulated sugar

1 tablespoon thinly sliced fresh mint

CITRUS GLAZE

2 cups confectioners' sugar

¼ cup fresh orange juice

¼ cup fresh lemon juice

1 quart lemon sherbet

Preheat the oven to 350° F. Butter and flour an 8½ × 4½-inch loaf pan, knocking out the excess flour.

Prepare the citrus pound cake: Combine the butter and sugar in an electric mixer fitted with the paddle attachment, and cream together on high speed, scraping the sides of the bowl as necessary, until the mixture is fluffy and light in color, 5 minutes. Add the lemon and orange zests and beat for 5 minutes. Add the eggs, one at a time, mixing well after each addition.

Sift the flour, baking powder, and salt together into a large bowl. In another bowl, combine the buttermilk and lemon juice. Add one third of the dry ingredients to the butter mixture, and mix until just incorporated. Add one third of the buttermilk mixture, and mix until just incorporated. Continue adding the dry and wet ingredients, being careful not to overmix and scraping down the sides of the bowl as needed. Pour the batter into the prepared loaf pan and bake for about 40 minutes, until the top is golden brown and a toothpick inserted into the center of the cake comes out clean. Cool in the pan.

Prepare the citrus compote: Holding the grapefruit in your hand over a bowl to collect the juices, run a sharp knife alongside the white membranes to remove the segments. Reserve the membranes and juice separately. Repeat with the remaining fruit, combining the segments and juices in the two bowls.

Place the Grand Marnier, sugar, and all the reserved juice in a medium saucepan and bring to a boil. Cook until the liquid is reduced to about ¼ cup, 12 minutes. Remove the pan from the heat and fold in the fruit segments and the mint.

Prepare the citrus glaze: Whisk all the ingredients together in a medium bowl.

Brush the glaze over the cake, letting it drip down the sides. Slice the pound cake, and serve it topped with lemon sherbet, with the compote spooned over all.

GRANDMA'S TOFFEE BARS

Tom Robey worked at Commander's Palace for almost twenty years. He was a beloved sous-chef (one of the best in country), full of talent and with a love of teaching new cooks the skills and tricks he'd learned in our busy kitchen. His wacky and nonstop humor helped us through many a hard time. We love Tom, and we love his Grandma's Toffee Bars.

• MAKES 24 BARS •

4 cups quick-cooking oats

1 cup packed light brown sugar

1 cup (2 sticks) unsalted butter, melted

1¼ cups smooth peanut butter

1¼ cups milk chocolate chips

1¼ cups butterscotch chips

Preheat the oven to 425°F.

Stir the oats, brown sugar, and melted butter together in a medium bowl. Transfer the mixture to a 9×13-inch baking dish, spreading it evenly and packing it lightly with the back of a spoon. Bake for 12 to 15 minutes, until lightly colored and bubbly. Cool in the baking dish on a wire rack for 15 minutes. (The crust will firm as it cools.)

In the top of a double boiler, or in a large bowl set over a pan of barely simmering water, combine the peanut butter and chocolate and butterscotch chips. Cook, stirring occasionally, until melted, about 15 minutes. Spread the hot chocolate mixture over the top of the oat crust. Let cool, still in the baking dish, at room temperature until firm and the chocolate is firm and set, about 2 hours. Cut into squares.

TORY SAYS . . .

Wow, are these good! But I can only handle one or two at a time.

Gingerbread Cupcakes with Molasses Frosting

Cupcakes just make us want to smile, and they travel well. Gingerbread and molasses are a sweet and spicy marriage made in heaven.

• MAKES 12 CUPCAKES •

1¼ cups all-purpose flour

1 teaspoon baking soda

1 teaspoon ground cinnamon

½ teaspoon ground nutmeg

Pinch of salt

¼ cup canola oil

¼ cup sugar

1 large egg

½ cup plus 2 tablespoons molasses

½ cup hot water

¾ cup cream cheese, at room temperature

¾ cup confectioners' sugar

2 tablespoons bourbon

Preheat the oven to 350°F. Add muffin liners to a 12-cup standard muffin pan.

In a bowl, whisk together the flour, baking soda, cinnamon, nutmeg, and salt. In the bowl of an electric mixer, beat together the oil, sugar, and egg. Beat in the ½ cup molasses and the hot water. Beat in the flour mixture until just combined and smooth. Pour the mixture into the muffin cups and bake for about 20 minutes, until a toothpick inserted in the center comes out clean. Transfer the pan to a wire rack to cool.

With an electric mixer, cream together the cream cheese and confectioners' sugar until light and fluffy. Beat in the remaining 2 tablespoons molasses and the bourbon. Spread this frosting over the cool muffins.

Upside-Up Cup Custards

Instead of the usual layer of caramel on traditional cup custard, or crème caramel, this version floats a thin layer of Louisiana cane syrup on top. If you're not a cane syrup lover, you can substitute warm honey or maple syrup.

• SERVES 4 •

2 cups heavy cream
5 large egg yolks
½ cup sugar

⅛ teaspoon vanilla extract
2 tablespoons Steen's pure cane syrup
    (see Resources, page 218)

Preheat the oven to 300°F. Arrange four 6-ounce ovenproof coffee cups or ramekins in a baking dish that is large enough to hold them without touching.

Bring the cream to a simmer in a medium saucepan over medium heat. Remove the pan from the heat.

Whisk the egg yolks and sugar in a bowl until thick and lemon colored, 2 to 3 minutes. Slowly whisk in ½ cup of the hot cream.

Return the saucepan to low heat and slowly whisk in the egg mixture. Cook, whisking constantly, until thick, 2 to 3 minutes. Strain the custard through a fine-mesh strainer into a bowl. Stir in the vanilla. Divide the custard among the cups and fill the baking dish with enough water to come halfway up the sides of the cups. Bake on the middle rack of the oven for 40 to 45 minutes, until the custards are set and the centers shake slightly.

Remove the custards from the water bath and transfer them to a wire rack to cool to room temperature.

Drizzle the cane syrup over the custards, and serve. (The custards can be made up to 1 day ahead; cover and refrigerate.) Warm the syrup before serving.

Tory Says . . .

The best way to eat this dish is with a contrast in temperature. Make sure the custard is near room temperature, and drizzle very warm cane syrup over it at the last second before you eat (you can microwave it). It will magically make you smile from ear to ear!

Resources

MAIL-ORDER SOURCES

Unfortunately, game is not always available at your local supermarket, so we've included some sources for it here, along with other sources for seafood and for local New Orleans and Louisiana ingredients.

ALLIGATOR MEAT

Bayou Land Seafood
Ask for Adam Johnson
www.bayoulandseafood.com
800-737-6868

Cajun Grocer
www.cajungrocer.com
888-CRAWFISH

Kajun Katfish
Ask for Joey Fonseca
985-758-7454

AMBERJACK

Samuels & Son Seafood Co.
www.samuelsandsonseafood.com
800-580-5810

ANDOUILLE SAUSAGE

Cajun Grocer
www.cajungrocer.com
888.CRAWFISH

Manda Packing Co.
www.mandafinemeats.com
800-343-2642

Paul Prudhomme Products
www.shop.chefpaul.com
800-457-2857

Racca's Specialty Meats
Ask for Butch Racca
337-558-4139 or
337-263-0025

BLACK BEAR

Exotic Meats
www.exoticmeats.com
800-680-4375

Venison America
www.venisonamerica.com
800-310-2360

BOUDIN

Hebert's Meats
www.hebertsmeats.com
918-298-8400

Racca's Specialty Meats
Ask for Butch Racca
337-558-4139 or
337-263-0025

BUFFALO

Big Valley Buffalo
www.bigvalleybuffalo.com
877-469-5756

Jackson Hole Buffalo Meat
www.buybuffalomeat.com
800-543-6328

CANE VINEGAR AND CANE SYRUP

Bayou Country
www.bayoucountry.com
888-571-3200

C. S. Steen's Syrup Mill
www.steensyrup.com
800-725-1654

The Vinegar Man
www.vinegarman.com

CATFISH

Kajun Katfish
Ask for Joey Fonseca
985-758-7454

CHANTERELLE MUSHROOMS

Foods in Season
www.foodsinseason.com
866-PORCINI

Fresh and Wild
www.freshandwild.com

CHEESE

Creole Cream Cheese
Smith Creamery
Mount Harman, LA
985-877-4445

CHOUPIQUE CAVIAR

Cajun Caviar
Ask for John Burke

www.cajuncaviar.com or johncaviar@
yahoo.com
504-813-3515

COBIA

Harlon's LA Fish
504-467-3809
nolrah@aol.com

New Orleans Fish House
www.NOFH.com
504-821-9700

COFFEE

French Market Coffee
504-581-7234

CONCH

Turks and Caicos Conch
www.cfarmsllc.com
305-362-5484

CRABMEAT

New Orleans Fish House
www.NOFH.com
504-821-9700

CRAWFISH

Bayou Land Seafood
www.bayoulandseafood.com
800-737-6868

Kyle LeBlanc Crawfish Farms
www.klcrawfishfarms.com
985-226-6444

Louisiana Crawfish Company
www.lacrawfish.com
888-522-7292

CREOLE MUSTARD

Zatarain's
www.zatarain.com

CRYSTAL HOT SAUCE

Cajun Grocer
www.cajungrocer.com
888-CRAWFISH

ELK

Exotic Meats
www.exoticmeats.com
800-680-4375

Jackson Hole Buffalo Meat
www.buybuffalomeat.com
800-543-6328

Venison America
www.venisonamerica.com
800-310-2360

FIG PRESERVES

Stonewall Preserves
www.stonewallkitchens.com
800-207-JAMS

FIVE-PEPPER JELLY

McIlhenny Company
www.TABASCO.com

FLORIDA LOBSTER

Triar Seafood Co.
Ask for Peter Jarvis
www.triarseafood.com
800-741-3474

FLOUNDER

New Orleans Fish House
www.NOFH.com
504-821-9700

Triar Seafood Co.
Ask for Peter Jarvis
www.triarseafood.com
800-741-3474

FOIE GRAS

D'Artagnan Foods
www.dartagnan.com
800-327-8246

Grimaud Farms
www.grimaud.com
800-466-9955

Hudson Valley
www.hudsonvalleyfoiegras.com
845-292-2500

FROG LEGS

Triar Seafood Co.
Ask For Peter Jarvis
www.triarseafood.com
800-741-3474

GOOSE

Exotic Meats
www.exoticmeats.com
800-680-4375

GRITS

Anson Mills
www.ansonmills.com
803-467-4122

GROUPER

Harlon's LA Fish
504-467-3809
nolrah@aol.com

New Orleans Fish House
www.NOFH.com
504-821-9700

HEIRLOOM TOMATOES AND SPECIALTY VEGETABLES

Rawfoodinfo.com
A search engine for healthy organic
specialty produce and tomatoes

HOG'S HEAD CHEESE

Bayou Boudin
Ask for Rocky or Lisa
www.bayoucabins.com
337-332-6158

Racca's Specialty Meats
Ask for Butch Racca
337-558-4139 or 337-263-0025

Mahimahi

New Orleans Fish House
www.NOFH.com
504-821-9700

Triar Seafood Co.
Ask for Peter Jarvis
www.triarseafood.com
800-741-3474

Maine Lobsters

Maine Lobster Direct
www.mainelobsterdirect.com
800-556-2783

Mako Shark

Santa Monica Seafood Company
www.santamonicaseafood.com

Triar Seafood Co.
Ask for Peter Jarvis
www.triarseafood.com
800-741-3474

Morel Mushrooms

Foods in Season
www.foodsinseason.com
800-222-5578

Oregon Mushroom Company
www.oregonmushrooms.com
800-682-0036

Gulf Oysters

Harlon's LA Fish
504-467-3809
nolrah@aol.com

New Orleans Fish House
www.NOFH.com
504-821-9700

P & J Oyster Company
Ask for Sal
www.oysterlover.com
888-LABAYOU

Pheasants and Quail

Exotic Meats
www.exoticmeats.com
800-680-4375

Popcorn Rice

Falcon Rice Mill Inc.
www.falconrice.com
800-738-7423

Cajun Supermarket
www.cajunsupermarket.com

Rabbit

Exotic Meats
www.exoticmeats.com
800-680-4375

RAINBOW TROUT

New Orleans Fish House
www.NOFH.com
504-821-9700

Pure Foods Fish Market
www.freshseafood.com
800-392-FISH

REDFISH

American Seafood
504-822-3983

New Orleans Fish House
www.NOFH.com
504-821-9700

SEA SCALLOPS

Gorton's of Gloucester
www.gortonsfreshseafood.com
800-335-3674

WILD LOUISIANA SHRIMP

New Orleans Fish House
www.NOFH.com
504-821-9700

SOFT-SHELL CRABS

Harbour House Crabs
www.ilovecrabs.com
888-458-8272

Kajun Katfish
Ask for Joey Fonseca
985-758-7454

New Orleans Fish House
www.NOFH.com
504-821-9700

SPECKLED TROUT

Harlon's LA Fish
504-467-3809
nolrah@aol.com

New Orleans Fish House
www.NOFH.com
504-821-9700

SUGARCANE SKEWERS

Louisiana Fresh Produce
504-309-7263

TASSO

Poche's
www.pochesmarket.com
800-3POCHES

Racca's Specialty Meats
Ask for Butch Racca
337-558-4139 or 337-263-0025

TRUFFLE OIL

Urbani U.S.A.
www.urbanitartufi.com
877-482-7883

VENISON

Broken Arrow Ranch
www.brokenarrowranch.com
800-962-4263

Venison America
www.venisonamerica.com
800-310-2360

WILD BOAR

Broken Arrow Ranch
www.brokenarrowranch.com
800-962-4263

Venison America
www.venisonamerica.com
800-310-2360

WILD RICE

Konriko Company Store
www.conradricemill.com
888-551-3245

WILD TURKEY

Exotic Meats
www.exoticmeats.com
800-680-4375

THE BEST GUIDES IN THE SOUTH AND BEYOND

If you want to enjoy some of the same fishing and hunting trips that we have over the years, here are some of our favorite guides plus Web sites for more information about contacting guides in your area.

FISHING

LOUISIANA

Theophile Bourgeois, Bourgeois Charters
(Coastal fishing)
www.neworleansfishing.com
504-341-5614

Poncho Hertz, Rajun Cajun
(Coastal fishing)
504-650-1918

Shane Mayfield
(Coastal fishing)
504-343-7388

James Peters, Ospray Charters
(Coastal and offshore fishing)
www.ospraycharters.com
985-727-1469

Anthony Randazzo
(Coastal fishing)
504-656-9940

Nash Roberts, Jr.
(Coastal fishing)
504-650-1918

FLORIDA

Captain Shawn Dahnke
(Offshore fishing)
dahnkesir@aol.com
850-837-3669

Flyliner Charters, Inc.
Pat Dineen
(Coastal and offshore fishing)
www.flyliner.com
850-609-0528 or 850-376-0400

Captain Bill Waitzman
850-837-6299 or 850-685-1952

COLORADO

Telluride Outside/Telluride Angler
(Catch-and-release trout fly-fishing)
www.tellurideoutside.com
800-831-6230

COSTA RICA

Costa Rican Dreams
(Sport fishing)
www.costaricadreams.com
011-506-637-8942 or 732-901-8625, ext. 46

SEARCH ENGINES FOR FISHING GUIDES

www.fishhoo.com (the Web site for guides nationwide)

www.charternet.com (for Florida Panhandle only)

www.ultimatefishingsite.com
www.huntingandfishingguides.net

HUNTING

LOUISIANA

Hackberry Rod and Gun Club
(Duck, goose, and alligator hunts)
www.hackberryrodandgun.com
888-762-3391

COLORADO

Colorado Hunting Expeditions
Dave Hill
(Elk, mule deer, and wild turkey hunts)
970-729-0270

TEXAS

Double Dime Ranch
(Venison and wild boar hunts)
www.doubledimeranch.com

Prairie Waterfowl Hunts
Davis Wadell
(Duck and goose hunts)
www.prairiewaterfowlhunts.com
979-758-4193

ARGENTINA

Estancia Los Chanares
David Denise
(Dove hunts)
888-850-HUNT, ext. 3

SEARCH ENGINES FOR HUNTING GUIDES

www.huntguide.com

www.huntingsociety.org

www.huntingtop10.com

www.huntingguidesandoutfitters.net

MORE HELPFUL WEB SITES

www.elkfoundation.org, The Elk Foundation, 866-455-7633

www.nwtf.org, The National Wild Turkey Federation, 800-THE-NWTF

www.pheasantcountry.com

Index

Olive Oil Meunière Sauce, 64–65

Roasted Pheasant with Cherry Glaze,
85–86

Pepper-Crusted Beef Sirloin with Crispy
Oysters and Horseradish Cream,
184–85

Peppers. *See* Chiles

Pheasant
Apple and Bourbon—Braised, 83–84
Pecan-Roasted, with Cherry Glaze, 85–86
size of, 83

Pie Dough, 70–71

Pies, Natchitoches Alligator, 70–71

Pineapple
and Wahoo, Grilled, Salad with Lime
Ginger Vinaigrette, 36–37
Wahoo and Tropical Fruit Skewers with
Coconut-Rum Dipping Sauce, 145–46

Pinot Noir Reduction, 28

Plantains
peeling, about, 197
Tostones (Fried Plantains), 197

Pompano
Crispy, with Spicy Cayenne Butter, 32–33
Grilled, with Orange Caramel Glaze,
34–35

Popcorn Balls, Spicy Praline-Crusted, 210

Pork. *See also* Andouille; Bacon; Sausages;
Tasso
Lemon and Garlic Grilled, 132
Loin, Coffee-Crusted, with Fig-Bourbon
Syrup, 131
Tory's Wild Game Sausage, 126–27
Wild Rice and Foie Gras Boudin, 87–88

Potato(es)
and Caramelized Onion Gratin, 204–5
Crawfish Boil, 154–55
Creole Cream Cheese Gnocchi with
Crawfish, 177–78
-Crusted Sheepshead with Smoked Tomato
Butter, 26–27
Marinated Crab Salad, 55
New, Creole Smashed, with Sour Cream,
Creole Mustard, and Green Onions, 198
Salad, Cajun, 194

Poultry. *See* Game birds

Praline-Crusted Popcorn Balls, Spicy, 210

Q

Quail
Grilled, with Wild Rice and Foie Gras
Boudin, 87–89
removing bones from, 88
Roasted, with Bourbon-Bacon Stuffing,
90–91
Stuffed, Coffee-Lacquered, 92–94

Quesadillas, Spicy Crawfish and Avocado, 153

R

Rabbit
Fried, Salad with Buttermilk—Black
Pepper Dressing, 112–13